Return of the Mexican Gray Wolf

Return

of the

Mexican Gray Wolf

Back to the Blue

Bobbie Holaday

The University of Arizona Press

Tucson

The University of Arizona Press
© 2003 Arizona Board of Regents
First Printing
All rights reserved
⊗ This book is printed on acid-free, archival-quality paper.
Manufactured in the United States of America

08 07 06 05 04 03 6 5 4 3 2 1

Library of Congress Cataloging-in-Publication Data

Holaday, Bobbie.
    Return of the Mexican gray wolf: back to the Blue/Bobbie Holaday.
    p. cm.
Includes bibliographical references and index.
    ISBN 0-8165-2295-2 (cloth : alk. paper)—ISBN 0-8165-2296-0
(pbk. : alk. paper)
    1. Mexican wolf—Arizona. 2. P.A.WS. (Group). 3. Wildlife
reintroduction—Arizona—Citizen participation. I. Title.

QL737.C22 H64 2003
639.97'977'09791—dc21

                                        2002153739

British Library Cataloguing-in-Publication Data
A catalogue record for this book is available from the British Library.

Publication of this book is made possible in part by a subsidy from the
Nongame Branch of the Arizona Game and Fish Department.

The author donates all royalties from the sale of this book to the Mexican
Wolf Trust Fund, administered by the Arizona Game and Fish
Department.

To Terry,

who made it happen,

and Jato,

who taught me the value

of now.

Contents

List of Illustrations

Color Photographs
Color photographs follow page 86

Val Asher using telemetry to monitor the wolves
Project staff loading Mexican wolves into panniers
Project staff loading pannier holding a wolf on mule's back
Wolves being carried from mules to a mesh pen
Wolves easily break out of mesh pens
Will Holder gathers his herd for pasture rotation
Captive pups

Black and White Photographs

Maps

Foreword

Restoration of wolves to parts of their former haunts is well accepted by the general public, and wolf restoration to Yellowstone National Park is the best-known such endeavor. Far fewer people are aware of the ongoing attempt to restore wolves to parts of the southwestern United States, notably eastern Arizona and western New Mexico. Although slightly different from the wolves restored to Yellowstone, the Mexican wolf (known to science as *Canis lupus baileyi*) is basically the same. Both are versions (subspecies, or geographic races) of the gray wolf *(Canis lupus)*. I say that they are "slightly different" because it takes a real expert, or a very close look at an animal's DNA, to distinguish a Mexican wolf from any other kind of wolf. No matter, though, for from a biological standpoint, the restoration of any wolf to its former range is momentous.

Biologically, restoring wolves is easy. Just drop off a few in an area with enough food—deer, elk, moose, sheep, goats, caribou, muskoxen, bison—and they will thrive. The problem comes when people enter the picture, and they always do. It turns out that in most areas to which wolves might be restored, some of the good citizens there hate wolves. After all, it has only been a few decades since they, their parents, or their grandparents did what they thought was their patriotic duty and got rid of all of them.

Among the many kinds of animals that wolves are adapted to prey upon are domestic livestock. In a frontier lifestyle, preventing wild creatures from killing your livestock was not just second nature, it was first and third as well. Thus not only did frontiersmen persecute the wolf, but so too did the federal government, and poison was the most efficient and effective method. By 1970, wolves were wiped out of every one of the forty-eight states except Minnesota, whose wilderness adjoined all of the Canadian wilderness, and of Isle Royale National Park, Michigan, also just south of the Canadian border.

Thus to local people with long memories or family traditions of despising predators, the idea of now trying to restore the wolf is anathema. This fact greatly complicates wolf restoration.

With the Mexican wolf, such a complicating factor is especially problematic. This is because the only Mexican wolves available for reintroducing into their former range are captive animals. All the other known Mexican wolves have been exterminated from the wild. During the last days of the extermination campaign, the U.S. government contracted a trapper to capture the last few and place them in captivity as potential breeding stock for a population that might later be used to try to restore the species in parts of its range. Without this effort there would have been no other source of Mexican wolves for any restoration effort. That's the good news.

The bad news is that using captive wolves as a source for restoring a population is doubly difficult. No matter what is done to try to prevent them from getting used to people, it is nowhere near enough. Captive-raised wolves just don't have the basic fear of humans that strikes terror in the hearts of wild wolves and makes them avoid any fresh sign of humans.

Thus captive wolves released into the wilds where their ancestors long ago roamed tend to spend too much time in the open, to frequent roads, and to haunt the local livestock grazing areas. This, of course, renders them vulnerable to any handy wolf-hater with a gun. And in the Mexican wolf reintroduction area, carrying a gun is almost mandatory.

It is no surprise, then, that restoring Mexican wolves to the Southwest is a much more difficult task than using wild wolves from Canada was to restore a wolf population to Yellowstone.

Nevertheless the Mexican wolf restoration effort is succeeding. Although many reintroduced Mexican wolves have been sacrificed on the altar of restoration, the population continues to increase, with several litters born in the wild every year. And that is momentous, a major accomplishment.

But the Mexican Wolf reintroduction did not just happen. It took years of planning and politicking, arguing and persuading, organizing and lobbying, prodding and poking. One of the prominent people doing this prodding and poking and organizing and lobbying was Bobbie Holaday. And now, in this book, she tells her story. It is a long and involved tale with many a heartbreak. It is also a heartening story and a satisfying one, for it shows not only what a dedicated citizen can do, but also demonstrates the great rewards, satisfactions, and accomplishments that persistence and the right motivation can bring.

Anyone interested in wolves and their recovery owe Bobbie a big "thank you" and "congratulations" for her long and successful dedication to this effort.

L. David Mech

Senior Research Scientist, Biological Resources
Division, U.S. Geological Survey, Northern Prairie,
Wildlife Research Center

Preface

Humanity has four and a half *billion* passionate advocates—but how many speak ... for the gray wolf? ... It is a man's duty to speak for the voiceless. A woman's obligation to aid the defenseless. Human needs do not take precedence over other forms of life; we must share this lovely, delicate, vapor-clouded little planet with all. And I quote: "For I say unto you, ... as you do to the least of these, so you do unto me."

—Edward Abbey, *Beyond the Wall*

I couldn't agree more. Edward Abbey, wherever you are, know that I am one of those advocates who did come to the aid of the defenseless and speak for the voiceless. In the pages that follow, I have recorded how I came to feel called to see the Mexican wolf return to the wilds of the Southwest and my eleven-year effort to help make it happen.

One person can make a difference. Today, many species are extinct due to humanity's selfish destruction of both species and habitat. Unless something is done to stop the rapid acceleration of species destruction, our grandchildren may know less than half the species we know today.

When I began this adventure back in 1988, I knew very little about wolves. It was a process of self-education. If you choose to support as controversial a project as I did, be prepared for plenty of conflict, opposition, and disappointment. Here in the Southwest, grazing, timber, and mining industries still control the legislative bodies. Politicians control decisions made by the wildlife agencies. While some agency staff members work diligently in support of wildlife and preservation of habitat, their striving may go for naught unless it can be clearly demonstrated that the majority of the public is on their side. I was naive enough to believe that all those men and women who work for wildlife agencies are totally driven by their desire to save wildlife, and that their motives must be pure. What a rude awakening I was to have.

Know this: Striving to save wildlife species and their dwindling habitats is a noble goal. It takes tremendous persistence in the face of those with money and power who want to expedite their short-range goals regardless of impacts on wildlife and habitat. You have moments on the mountaintops of exhilaration, and moments in the desolate valleys of despair. You have days when the goal you have set out to pursue appears absolutely impossible to achieve. But you must persist. God did not create a single unnecessary species, and although God gave humanity the responsibility of stewardship over all other living things, God did not give us the right to slash, burn, and slaughter.

I have been asked many times why I was so sure the Mexican wolf would be eventually returned to the wild. My reply was always, "Because it's so damn right!"

Acknowledgments

I hope the following includes everyone to whom I owe thanks for helping me with this book on the return of the Mexican wolves to the Blue.

From the Arizona Game and Fish Department: Terry Johnson, Bill Van Pelt, Frosty Taylor, Val Asher, Dan Groebner, Rich Remington, Stephanie Naftal, Alexis Watts, Karen Schedler, Joanne Kirchner, Kerry Baldwin, and Heidi Vasiloff.

From the Arizona Game and Fish Commission: Tom Woods, Beth Woodin, Art Porter, and Mike Golightly.

From the U.S. Forest Service: Larry Allen, Don Hoffman, Peggy Gladhill, Frank Hayes, Bob Dyson, and Leon Fisher.

From the U.S. Fish and Wildlife Service: Michael Spear, David Parsons, Diane Boyd-Heger, Wendy Brown, Brian Kelly, Michelle Brown, and Paul Morey.

From the AGRO Land and Cattle Company: Dan and Mary Bates.

From Defenders of Wildlife: Hank Fischer, Rodger Schlickeisen, Nina Fascione, Bob Ferris, Craig Miller, Minette Johnson, Mary Beth Beetham, Evan Hirsche, and Caroline Kennedy.

From the Sierra Club: Joni Bosh, Rob Smith, Renee Guillory, and Sandy Bahr.

From the Audubon Society: Dave Henderson, Bob Witzeman, and Charles Babbitt.

From the Center for Biodiversity: Robin Silver.

From the Phoenix Zoo: Jeff Williamson, Annette Heath, John Vack, Becky Adams, Mike Seidman, Mike Demlong, and Terri Volk.

From the Turner Endangered Species Fund: Mike Phillips.

From the Red Wolf Project: Warren Parker.

Authors: Rick McIntyre, Rita Robinson, Brenda Peterson, Stephanie Lyncheski, and Louise De Wald.

P.A.WS. members: David Bluestein, Gary Wheat, Patty Williams, Tammy and Merle Anderson, Will Stefanov, Meg Hendrick, Barbara Boltz, June Payne, Jennifer Donovan, Melinda Butler, Jay Nochta, Tom Hulen, Ann DeJong Ruhneau, Chris Rossie, Donna Storie, John Engle, Diana Pfaff, Bill Chamberlain, Wanda Winningham, and Don Wilson.

Other friends of the Mexican wolf: Vicki O'Toole, Liz Sizemore, Grove Burnett, Toxie Beavers, Marcia Sullivan, Pam Kelly, Cindy Roper, Brian Cobble, Susan Larson, and Carol Martindale.

From Wolf Haven International: Jack Laufer, Beth Church, and Julie Palmquist.

From the International Wolf Center: Dave Mech, Walter Medwig, and Mary Ortiz.

Rancher friends: Jim, Clarice, Jan, and Will Holder; Clay and Karen Riggs; Ruken Jelks III; Alan and Diana Kessler; Barbara and Bill Marks; Pat and Raymond Cline; Roxanne Knight; and Tommie Martin.

From the Arizona-Sonora Desert Museum: Carol Cochran and Peter Siminski.

From Native Ecosystems: Steve Johnson.

From the University of Arizona Press: Christine Szuter, Nancy Arora, Anne Keyl, Yvonne Reineke, and Melanie Mallon.

To any others I've forgotten, my apologies and thanks.

Return of the Mexican Gray Wolf

Back to the Blue—and Before

It is an arrogant assumption to say that human beings are lords and masters of the lower creatures. On the contrary, being endowed with greater things in life, they are the trustees of the lower animal kingdom.... A society can be judged by the way it treats its animals.

—Mahatma Gandhi

"I saw a wolf near my house yesterday," said Don Hoffman. I had stopped by the U.S. Forest Service (USFS) Alpine Ranger Station to see Hoffman on my June 1998 camping trip to the Luna Lake campground east of Alpine. I had known him since the mid-1980s, when I frequently hiked in the Blue. Within the vast White Mountains in eastern Arizona, the area that includes the town of Alpine and the mountains and valleys that continue south to Clifton is known as the Blue Range Area, or just "the Blue." I had hiked nearly every trail in the upper Blue and had reported trail conditions to Hoffman, who was the field foreman for wilderness trails before his promotion to the Forest Service's local manager of wilderness trails and special forest uses.

Hoffman began his career with the USFS in Alpine in 1976. In 1977, he and his wife, Jane, bought land and built their home near the Blue River, deep in the heart of the Blue. They have lived there since, raising their two children, Karl and Gretchen. Don Hoffman epitomizes the old school of forestry that believes wilderness is best managed by nature, not by humans.

"That's fantastic!" I replied excitedly. "Did you ever really think this day would come?"

"Not really," he answered.

"Have you heard them howl at night?"

"No, I haven't. But my neighbor, who's a rancher, has heard them a couple of times."

"Did he seem upset about wolves being out there?"

"No, not at all. He sounded pretty excited about hearing them. So far, the wolves haven't killed any cattle, but apparently they have killed a rancher's dog. And I believe he accepted compensation from Defenders of Wildlife."

After talking with Hoffman, I rejoined my large traveling companion, Jato, my wolf-dog, for the drive east to Luna Lake. This Forest Service recreation site is in the eastern foothills of Escudilla Mountain.

The June air was cool and crystalline, and as I neared Luna Lake, the sunlight flung a gossamer sheath of gold over its ripples. I recalled how I had come to have a wolf-dog as a companion animal. About a year after my retirement from Honeywell in 1986, I was looking for a new dog. A good friend, hearing that I was considering a malamute, asked me why I didn't try a wolf-dog. Like most people who acquire wolf-dogs, I knew nothing of the behavior of a wolf.

After adopting my first wolf-dog pup, Luke, I soon adopted another, Jato, with little idea of what I was letting myself in for. Most wolf-dog owners choose Alaskan names for their pets, but my name choices were derived from Lukachukai and Oljato, favorite spots on the Navajo tribal reservation. It wasn't long before I realized that these pups were unlike any dogs I had owned in the past.

I read every book about wolves I could lay my hands on to learn more about why they behave the way they do. I joined a wolf-dog club to learn more about how wolf-dog owners cope with wolfish canine behavior.

Who would have guessed that one wolf-dog club meeting would so drastically redirect my retirement? In January 1988,

Terry Johnson, Nongame and Endangered Wildlife Program manager for the Arizona Game and Fish Department (AGFD), spoke to the club about the demise of the Mexican wolf. He told about the past history and background of the Mexican wolf and how efforts had been started to bring it back.

Johnson said the AGFD had participated in the early stages of the U.S. Fish and Wildlife Service (USFWS) proposed recovery program. He told us that the Department's involvement began in 1982 when David Brown, former game branch manager, and he had searched northern Mexico for thick-billed parrots, grizzly bears, and ridge nose rattlesnakes. They found parrots and ridge noses, but grizzlies were long gone. So was the wolf. They wondered whether the wolf could, or should, ever be restored to the landscape.

The following year, the Department hired Johnson to head its newly established Nongame and Endangered Wildlife Program. Wolf recovery was still on his mind, and the subject soon turned serious. In the spring of 1986, USFWS Regional Director Michael Spear, prompted by Johnson's discussions with his staff, asked Department Director Bud Bristow to help explore the possibility of reintroducing Mexican wolves into the Southwest. Bristow agreed to do so, but because of the complexities in establishing workable reintroduction procedures, progress stalled. Opposition to reintroducing Mexican wolves was strong, and no organized support existed in Arizona. In addition, there was interagency concern over the reports that Mexican wolves might exist along the Arizona-Mexico border. What could the implications of a single wolf in Arizona under full protection of the Endangered Species Act (ESA) have on efforts to reintroduce Mexican wolves under the nonessential-experimental classification of the ESA? Johnson told us that Mexican wolf recovery was going nowhere.

I'd long been an environmentalist, directing most of my efforts toward the designation of wilderness areas in Arizona.

I had also worked with the USFS on public-land grazing issues, often joining interdisciplinary teams to discuss allotment-management plans for various Arizona grazing allotments, many of which included acres of wilderness. But what was wilderness without the very essence of wildness—the wolf?

I asked Johnson whether it would make a difference if there were an organized group of advocates in Arizona supporting Mexican wolf reintroduction. He responded, "It sure wouldn't hurt."

His answer affected the next eleven years of my life.

As I neared Luna Lake campground, I remembered another camping trip, during the summer of 1988, when I'd first introduced my wolf-dogs to Don Hoffman and mentioned that I was planning to organize a group to support the Mexican wolf recovery program.

"It will never happen here," Hoffman had warned as we sat in my camper drinking coffee. "Jane and I have encountered a lot of hostility ever since it became known that we favored wilderness designation of the Blue Primitive Area. Jane used to get invited to the local Cowbelles' events, but when the ranchers found out we favored wilderness, they cut off her invitations."

"The wolves have a right to run free," I insisted. "There's only thirty-some now in captivity, and they may be gone in Mexico. Unless they are given a chance for freedom, we may end up with a captive animal too altered to survive in the wild."

"It would be great to have wolves in the Blue," Hoffman agreed. "When Jane and I decided to build our home down in the Blue, we knew we'd be exposing our family to lions and bears. We've learned to live with all wildlife and provide protection for our horses and dogs. Wolves sure wouldn't give us or anyone else in the Blue any more of a problem than lions do."

Survey upon survey has revealed overwhelming support for healthy wildlife populations. No wildlife population missing a major species like the wolf can be considered healthy. Robbed of the forest's most efficient predator, the increasing populations of elk had ranchers screaming for higher hunting permit numbers and longer hunting seasons. But they would not buy into the idea that wolves legally could kill elk year-round. Wolves belonged in the Blue.

Much of the local population harbored the medieval myths about the supernatural evil tendencies of wolves. These tales depicted a demonic beast that could slaughter a hundred head of livestock in a night, kill humans, and gobble up any children whom it happened to encounter. The early Anglo settlers brought legends into this vast wilderness, depicting the wolf as a sinister adversary, and in many local communities these same legends live on today. (Further background on folklore surrounding the wolf can be found in *Vanishing Lobo*, by James C. Burbank.)

Then, in the summer of 1998, the Mexican wolves were back. Earlier that year, on January 26, 1998, with much hype and hoopla, three Mexican wolves were carried to the Campbell Blue acclimation pen to begin a nine-week preconditioning period before release to the wild. Soon after the initial wolf transfer, a pair of wolves was placed in the Turkey Creek pen, and a family of six wolves into the Hawk's Nest pen with no fanfare. On March 29, 1998, all eleven wolves were quietly released from their pens, and once again the Blue Range Area echoed with the song of wolves' howls.

The history of the Mexican wolves' return has never been fully recorded, and I promised myself that I would write this story. During my visits to the Blue, I frequently sought out old-timers who could tell me about the early days. By learning about the history of the hardy settlers and grasping their perspectives,

I could better understand why the fourth- and fifth-generation residents resent what they consider outside interference with their communities' culture and customs.

From the archives at the Forest Service district office in Alpine, I learned that the first culture to inhabit this area were the Mogollon, hunters and gatherers, who occupied southwestern New Mexico and southeastern Arizona between 2,000 B.C. and A.D. 1,400. They were probably driven out by the Apaches by the time Francisco Vasquez de Coronado and his expedition explored the area in 1540, in search of the fabled Seven Cities of Cibola. Coronado found mud rather than gold, and the area remained in obscurity for many years.

In about 1825, mountain man and fur trapper James Ohio Pattie explored the area, searching for animals to trap. He found plenty of beaver but disliked what he described as jungles of the canyons' dense vegetation.

From Alpine's Bear Wallow Cafe menu, I learned that Anderson Bush first settled in Alpine in 1876. The area was then known as Bush Valley. In 1879, Mormon settlers were sent into the area, and two of them traded Bush a wagon team of mules and a saddle horse for Bush's rights to the area. Because the San Francisco River flows through the area, it was for a short time named Frisco. Later settlers renamed the town Alpine because of the alpine nature of the countryside.

To quote from the menu, "These industrious pioneers set to farming the area and building homes. Many died from hardships encountered and a few more were slain by marauding Indians. A fort was built east of town for protection. Some of the logs and stones from the old Bush Valley Fort were used in construction of some of the older houses in Alpine, which are still inhabited today." A monument has been erected east of town on State Route 180 that reads, "Here Stood The Old Bush Valley Fort For Protection Against Renegade Apaches."

Early Graham County sod-rooted homestead. Photo courtesy of the Graham County Historical Society.

Greenlee County, named for Mason Greenlee, an early prospector who settled in Clifton in 1874, was formed officially from a part of Graham County and legislated as the youngest county when Arizona achieved statehood in 1912. The Homestead Act of 1862 was intended to induce settlement, cultivation, and establishment of homes on public lands in the West. Homesteaders filed a notarized affidavit at the Office of Records, staked out the land, and filed a Homestead Entry Survey. The fee was $1.25 per acre. They were required to live on the land for three years before the final application for a deed, or "patent," would be filed.

During Alpine's settlement, all of the country we now know as the Blue Range Area was being settled by ranchers, mainly from Texas, traveling in covered wagons and driving herds of livestock. These ranchers had heard about the pristine grasslands in the high country and in the deep valleys along the Black and the Blue Rivers. The settlers found lush meadows of blue grama and Kentucky bluegrass in high mountain meadows and forests made up of ponderosa pine, blue spruce, and aspen mixed with Douglas and white fir trees. By 1929, the county boasted many herds of sheep, goats, and cattle. The forest was full of game animals, including turkeys and mule and white-tail deer.

Joseph Garrison Pearce, born in 1874, was Arizona's first forest ranger. *Arizona Memories* (Morgan and Strickland 1984) recorded Pearce's words in the following excerpts, which set the tone for the early days:

> My most important duty as the first forest ranger in Arizona, then as now, was fighting fires. But in April 1899, when I was appointed, the chief cause of fires wasn't the stub of a cigarette or a careless campfire, but the intent and purpose of the Apache Indians, whose reservation bordered on the Black Mesa Forest. They set the fires deliberately for the smoke. They had a sincere belief or superstition that smoke would bring rain. And in the driest seasons, when the forest was all ready to burn like tinder, up would pop a bit fire near the boundary of the reservation. And you couldn't catch them at it. . . .
>
> That was a great stretch of timber I patrolled, alone at first, and then with several rangers under me and a title as chief ranger. It was the largest stretch of untouched virgin timber in the United States, and so reported to President Roosevelt by Gifford Pinchot of Pennsylvania, who was then chief United States forester under the original Roosevelt and who inspected the forest with me while I was ranger. My territory included land from Flagstaff east to the New Mexico line, and from Springerville south to Clifton, a stretch larger than a couple of those New England states. . . .
>
> It was part of my work to estimate the number of sheep and cattle using the forest and collect the government fee for

grazing privileges. But the hard-bitten sheep and cattlemen couldn't get this new idea into their heads and regarded the land as theirs. They weren't even willing to secure the proper permit for grazing privileges.

Many times I've come on close-packed flocks using forest land and have ordered them off, and more often than not they refused to go, the owners claiming the land had been theirs for forty years and they'd be damned if they'd give it up now, government or no government. When this happened it was my duty to report them to my head, W. H. Buntam, forest superintendent at Santa Fe, New Mexico, and secure warrants for their arrests. A few arrests and trials, with stiff fines, began to make the stockmen change their minds.

There was a bearded old-timer, a sheepman and a nester in a little shack on government lands. I went up to his shack peaceable enough for the third time.

"Come in," he says to my knock. He was cooking breakfast when I went in, looked me over scowling, went back to his cooking. "It's you again! What's on your mind this time, young feller?"

I told him, "Just wanted to make a little collection for the Government on your sheep. I'll need to make a little roundup to count 'em."

He turned around then, eyes on fire, and braced heavy on the flats of both feet. "You see the door there?"

"Sure I see it."

"Know what it's for?"

"Reckon so."

"Listen here, young feller, I pay the Territory and the County taxes on my sheep and goats. I'd like to see the color of a man's hair that'll make me pay my taxes twice in Arizona. You see that door?"

"I seen it already." I said. "I judge you want me to use it." I walked outside and he followed me and stood in the doorway. "I'm coming back," I told him, "and when I come there'll be ten rangers with me, and we'll round you up."

"Like hell you will!" He slammed the door shut.

But I returned with two other rangers and a warrant

for arrest, and in the end he paid the fee—about eighty cents per sheep—and in addition a stiff fine. There wasn't any more trouble collecting from him after that.....

Besides fighting fires and collecting range fees and helping settle disputes, I had other jobs as a forest ranger, everyday jobs. Blazing trails, posting fire notices, marking timber to be cut.....

When Pinchot came for his inspection of the Black Mesa Forest, I took him along a trail I'd blazed some time before beyond Alpine southward toward Clifton. We came to the place the Blue Range breaks off almost sheer, and down below the mountains roll away toward Clifton.

Pinchot said, "Guess we'll have to turn around and go back. We can't get down off this mountain, Joe."

Then I told him I'd blazed the trail down there so that a rider could get through to Clifton. To prove it, we went down, leading our horses.

That evening in camp I asked him, "Do you think there'll ever be a wagon road there, down the Blue Range to the flats?"

He got a laugh out of that. "There'll never even be a good horse trail," he said. "The only way a man'll ever get down there easily is to grow wings and fly down."

That was forty years ago. And now every day automobiles go along through there and roll down the slopes of the Blue Range following almost exact the trail I blazed in 1899, now the Coronado Trail. (127, 131–132, 134)

Today that trail is Arizona State Route 191, originally designated as Route 666. The satanic connotation surrounding "666" irked the local citizenry, who reportedly requested the change in the route designation.

One of the first ranches in Arizona was the Double Circle Ranch, which stood at an elevation of five thousand feet. In 1880, George H. Stevens started it as a sheep ranch. The ranch once

Rounding up the Double Circle cattle, 1905. Photo courtesy of the Arizona Historical Society (#24775).

extended from the Black River through Eagle Creek and much of what would become the San Carlos Apache Indian Reservation over to Bylas. Early accounts of forest conditions estimate that Stevens may have grazed as many as one hundred thousand sheep at one time. Joe Hampson, who grazed about thirty thousand cattle and employed twenty to thirty cowboys, later purchased the ranch. By 1904, water was getting scarce and agriculture was beginning to decline. Cattle numbers decreased to about nine thousand head.

During the 1930s, when the first reservation lines were drawn, they mainly followed Eagle Creek. Portions to the east of Eagle Creek eventually became allotments for Anglo ranchers, and to the west the Department of the Interior administered the land for the Apaches. Employed by the Interior, John

Mack Hughes was transferred from Oraibi on the Hopi Reservation in May 1944 to Point of Pines to oversee grazing on the San Carlos tribal ranch. He held that position for nineteen years. Mack's wife, Stella, told me that in 1936, the Bureau of Indian Affairs closed all Anglo leases to the Double Circle Ranch and issued them to the Associations of Apache Cattlemen. Stella Hughes authored the award-winning book *Hashknife Cowboy,* which relates the history of her husband's experiences on the early frontier.

Hughes told me of having to tow a trailer carrying nine or ten head of cattle over the eighteen miles of dirt road from Eagle Creek to Point of Pines in dreadful weather, when this road "was a real bitch." "Earning a living under these rustic conditions was really hard. You just got used to it," she told me. She said that, in the early days, wolves ranged widely in that area. "Government wolfers" trapped most of them from the reservation before the 1940s because the wolves were "terribly destructive." Hughes said, "I saw one picture of a barn on the Double Circle with eight or ten wolves nailed to the outside wall."

During 1944, a government trapper from Miami, Arizona, was hired to trap the few remaining wolves running between Black River and the Nantez Rim. Stella Hughes was with Mack when the trapper caught the last three they ever saw for ten years. But she added that in the mid-1950s, "Two crossed in front of us at about midnight, halfway between Point of Pines and Black River Dam on Phelps/Dodge property, and there was never any doubt about what we saw."

The Double Circle Ranch is important to our story because of the Holder family at Anchor Ranch on Eagle Creek, who now support wolf recovery. All the land comprising the Anchor Ranch was once a part of the huge Double Circle. Clarice Holder

Eugene Cleveland Holder (right) with unidentified hunter.
Photo courtesy of Pat Cline and Chris Rossie.

is the wife of Jim Holder, and mother of Will Holder, who now operates this ranch with his wife, Jan. Clarice believed that her grandfather, James Hicks, once worked on the Double Circle.

James Hicks had come west from Texas in 1918 and settled at Eagle Creek. He purchased the ranch now known as the Baseline allotment from a gentleman who had homesteaded the ranch.

John Francis Holder, grandfather of Jim Holder, was born in Mississippi in 1846. Jim Holder says his grandfather was a real character and once served as a character witness for Billy the Kid in New Mexico before coming to Arizona.

One of John's sons, Eugene Cleveland, was born on March 4, 1888, the same day that President Grover Cleveland took office. Eugene Cleveland Holder and his third wife, Helen Walker Wilbanks, were Jim Holder's parents. Eugene Holder worked as a game warden for the AGFD, and the killing of wolves, bears, lions, and coyotes was common in those days. He is credited with killing the last wolf in the Mogollon country in about 1932. He had the hide made into a fur stole for his youngest sister, Mae. Mae Holder, who married Walter Haught, kept the wolf stole until her death in the early 1990s. The wolf stole is now in the possession of her daughter, Pat Haught Cline of Star Valley, who with her husband, Raymond, operated the 7A Ranch.

Eugene Holder's son, Jim, married Clarice Hicks in 1960 and for a time lived in Flagstaff before purchasing the current Baseline allotment from Greenwade in 1967. The Baseline and nearby Horse Springs allotments have been managed as the Anchor Ranch since 1991, when Jim and Clarice Holder bought the Hicks Ranch.

In 1995, Will and Jan Holder named their first-born son Cleve after Jim Holder's father, Eugene Cleveland Holder. Will Holder jokingly told me he is repaying his karmic debt in that he hopes his son will make up for any damages to the wildlife populations that his grandfather may have caused.

During another trip to the Blue, I met an elderly resident of Springerville whose perspectives on wolves and predators reflected that of many of the old-time foresters, game managers, sportsmen, and livestock operators in that area. This man declined my request to use his name.

In the mid-1880s, his grandparents had settled and set up a ranching operation in New Mexico on lands now included in the Gila National Forest. He said neither he nor his father encountered wolves, but his grandfather had lost livestock to one of the last wolves in the area when they were preparing to drive the cattle for shipment.

He'd heard tales of how wolves would hamstring and gut a lot of cattle and horses. He believed that wolves would kill just for the fun of it and commented that the people who want wolves back may believe that they are beautiful and cuddly animals, but wolves are really destructive predators. He thought wolves are like the killers in penitentiaries and should never be turned loose to kill again because they would totally decimate the deer herds for future generations. He asked me if I wanted to trade the deer for the wolves and told me that all of us who were so anxious to see wolves return should think twice about what we were doing.

Other accounts of early settlers local people told me recalled the difficulties encountered in their daily living, under harsh conditions with no running water or electricity. They did enjoy closely knit community ties among the rural folk, but they shared a bitter resentment of the federal government's interference with their way of life. They maintained a righteous attitude toward the killing of any predator that they believed threatened their livestock and their own personal safety. Today, fourth- and fifth-generation ranchers cannot accept the public-land concept and still feel that the land is rightfully theirs. They insist that the local folk, not federal authorities, should make decisions about their grazing operations and about wildlife.

Except for ranchers like the Holders, most of the Blue Range Area descendants of the old-timers despise predators, particularly wolves. It is against this background that the federal and state agencies, with the support of wolf advocates, brought the Mexican wolves back to the Blue.

2

The Calling and the Challenge

He prayeth best, who loveth best
All things both great and small,
For the dear God who loveth us
He made and loveth all.

—Samuel Taylor Coleridge, "The Rime of the Ancient Mariner"

I have always "blamed" Terry Johnson for my decision, in 1988, to take on the reintroduction of the Mexican wolf as my retirement project. How could I overlook this animal, placed on Earth for a purpose, but whose predator role had been so badly maligned? The Mexican wolf couldn't speak for itself. Someone had to be its voice. Following the January 1988 wolf-dog club meeting, I told Johnson of my decision to establish a group to provide support for the Arizona Game and Fish Department's (AGFD's) efforts on behalf of the Mexican wolf.

Johnson earned his bachelor's degree in biology at Central State College in Oklahoma and his master's in ecology at Stephen F. Austin State University in Texas; his doctorate in wildlife ecology at the University of Arizona is near completion. He is basically an evolutionary ecologist who took a right turn into conservation work with the Arizona state government. Throughout the coming years, Terry Johnson would be my mentor.

Johnson provided me with many public documents, including the original Mexican Wolf Recovery Plan and past correspondence between staff from the AGFD and the U.S. Fish and Wildlife Service (USFWS). Staff at the USFWS Albuquerque office also sent me many additions to my growing library on the Mexican wolf.

Settlers waged all-out war against wolves. Photo courtesy of the U.S. Fish and Wildlife Service.

From these documents, I learned that Mexican wolves and humans had been in conflict from the time the early settlers arrived. As settlers struggled to tame the wilds and make a living in the American Southwest, they often disrupted well-established ecological patterns. The settlers moved onto lands that since Pleistocene times had been the homes and hunting grounds of a variety of predators. The settlers cut down forests, farmed the floodplains, and grazed the grass and shrublands with much livestock. Existing at a near-subsistence level, many settlers were forced to live off the game animals.

The combination of much reduced game populations and tremendous numbers of livestock placed the owners in a bitter clash with predators. By the early 1900s, predators, including the wolf, preyed on ranging livestock. Stockmen, fearing for their personal and economic well-being, declared all-out war on the

Lone wolves were trapped. Photo courtesy of the U.S. Fish and Wildlife Service.

Mexican wolf. Wolf eradication became a crusade to the livestock industry, which united and, through powerful political forces, government support, and efficient methods, succeeded in a few decades in removing Mexican wolves from the American Southwest.

This did not happen in a vacuum, and cattlemen alone should not be blamed for the extirpation of the wolf. No group or organization opposed their single-minded purpose. No voice was raised for a more controlled program. On the contrary, most sentiment was in favor of wolf elimination. Only in the last few decades have we heard voices raised in defense of wolves.

By the 1930s, only a few transient wolves remained. The last reported wolf carcass in New Mexico was found in October 1970, in the Peloncillo Mountains. In December 1970, the only (and last) authenticated wolf kills from Texas were reported.

The first was killed by a hunter, the second trapped. By the 1970s, attitudes were changing, and many biologists and members of the public began to realize the mistake that earlier generations had made by wiping out the wolves. An era of ecology was just dawning.

In 1973, the Endangered Species Act (ESA) was signed by the U.S. Congress, and the Mexican wolf was designated as a threatened subspecies by the U.S. Bureau of Sport Fisheries and Wildlife (later the U.S. Fish and Wildlife Service [USFWS]). In 1976, the USFWS issued a Proposed Rule in the Federal Register listing *Canis lupus baileyi* as an endangered species. Soon after, the Mexican wolf was listed as endangered under the ESA.

Later that year, Arizona's Aravaipa wolf was killed by a private trapper for a reputed bounty of $500, put up by local ranchers. Biologists who examined the skull indicated the animal was a true wolf. The wolf had been killed after it had been declared endangered, but the USFWS would not confirm the animal as a wolf. Their records still list the 1970 killings of wolves in New Mexico and Texas as the last wolves killed, but the Aravaipa wolf was probably the last Mexican wolf to be taken in the Southwest.

In 1979, the USFWS established a cooperative agreement with the government of Mexico to address the possibility of recovering the Mexican wolf. At that time, there were only four wild-caught-confirmed Mexican wolves in captivity at the Arizona-Sonora Desert Museum (ASDM). All of these animals had been captured in Mexico by Roy McBride of Alpine, Texas, under a contract issued by the USFWS. Roy had a keen sense of wolf behavior, having previously tracked, trapped, and shot many wolves in response to ranchers' complaints of wolf depredation on cattle. The Mexican government had arranged the necessary permits for the capture and export of the animals for the purpose of establishing an official captive breeding program. McBride's records showed that the first male was captured in December 1972. It died before making any genetic contribution. The second wolf, captured in 1977, eventually made genetic contributions to the program. Both were captured near Durango, Mexico. Another male was captured near Chihuahua, but he died before making any contribution to the program.

In March 1978, McBride captured a male and female traveling together near Durango. The female was heavy with pups and later delivered four male pups and one female pup in May of 1978 at the Arizona-Sonora Desert Museum (ASDM). It is possible that the male traveling with the pregnant female sired the pups. However, he died in captivity in 1981 at the ASDM, making no further genetic contributions. In 1980, McBride captured a sixth Mexican wolf, a male, in Chihuahua. In May 1981, this male wolf, with the previously caught wild female, produced a litter at the Wild Canid Survival and Research Center at Eureka, Missouri. These wolves started what is now called the certified, or the McBride, lineage of Mexican wolves.

Another group of captive Mexican wolves originally housed at the ASDM was later known as the Ghost Ranch lineage. Private citizens captured the founding male near Tumacacori, Arizona, in 1959. Other individuals captured the founding female as a pup in Sonora, Mexico, in 1961. The same people later took these wolves to the ASDM, where they were cared for by the ASDM staff for several years. The pair gave birth to at least four pups at the ASDM during the 1960s. This lineage was later dispersed to different captive facilities in Arizona and New Mexico. Another lineage, known as the Aragon lineage, had existed since the 1960s at the Aragon Zoo in Mexico City. Neither of these two lineages was originally certified as pure, nor were the wolves bred with the McBride line for some years, during which DNA tests were run by forensic laboratories to ascertain the purity of their blood lines.

In 1979, the USFWS, now mandated to recover this endangered subspecies, put together the Mexican Wolf Recovery Team.

A founder of the Mexican Wolf Captive-Breeding Program. Photo by Tom Smylie, U.S. Fish and Wildlife Service.

The original team included Norma Ames, of the New Mexico Department of Game and Fish, as team leader; Larry Allen, range coordinator for the Coronado National Forest, U.S. Forest Service (USFS); Gary Nunley, of the USFWS; Jose C. Trevino, Dirección General de la Fauna Silvestre of Mexico; and Peter Siminski and Dr. Ingeborg Poglayen, both of the ASDM, among its members. Team members contributed to the Mexican Wolf Recovery Plan, published in 1982, authored by Norma Ames on behalf of the USFWS.

The AGFD's early participation during 1986 through 1988 in the wolf program is detailed in an informal summary Terry Johnson wrote in 1995, portions of which follow:

> No other animal native to the Southwest has been so hated as the Mexican wolf, and for many this hatred still exists, although to a large extent the attitude toward wolves in the Southwest has changed during the latter quarter of the 20th century.
>
> The Service began the effort by meeting with various agencies in Albuquerque, New Mexico, on 26 June 1986. Participants included representatives from the states of Arizona, New Mexico, and Texas, and the USFS. Discussion focused on what constituted historic range for the Mexican wolf; how to identify areas that would merit detailed evaluation as potential reintroduction sites; and how project information should be released to the public. Several sites were discussed, but no specific areas were identified for detailed evaluation. More importantly, no plans were made for a coordinated public information effort.
>
> After the Albuquerque meeting, Fish and Wildlife (14 July 1986) asked each state to identify areas that had potential as reintroduction sites. Since Texas was precluded by state law from reintroducing wolves, only Arizona and New Mexico responded. Arizona Game and Fish conducted an internal review, and identified fifteen areas in Arizona that seemed to meet the selection criteria and merit further consideration. Before submitting the list, the Department again asked Fish and Wildlife to begin informing the public about

what was (and was not) being discussed. The Service declined, stating it was too soon to do so.

The Department remained concerned about the effects of unplanned disclosure to the public. Unfortunately, the issue had already been leaked, and the media quickly turned to Recovery Team members willing to discuss it. The news coverage indicated cooperators were well down the road to reintroduction. That was simply not true, but given how the story broke, a stigma of distrust and predetermined outcome was already attached to the issue.

Dissatisfied with the disorganized and initially secretive Federal approach to evaluating wolf reintroduction, and the public distrust that approach helped generate, the Department began developing a more orderly process, now known as the "Arizona 12-step."

On October 9, 1986, a letter from Terry Johnson to Jim Johnson, chief of endangered species for USFWS Region 2, summarized the AGFD's proposed plan for the reintroduction:

> The Department has drafted reintroduction procedures that provide specific guidelines for all wildlife reintroductions.... We expect this document will facilitate performing the next phase of wolf reintroduction, which involves: 1) defining specific boundaries within which the release and initial wolf wanderings might occur, and 2) coordinating with local land management agencies,...
>
> The second action regarding coordination is of paramount importance. Our proposed strategy will likely include contacting all involved public and private entities to insure that they have a voice in the process while it is occurring, not after release area boundaries and priorities are established. This coordination will take about six months to complete, thus setting July 1987 as the time by which we will have specific release areas defined, if any can be defined.

Jim Johnson agreed with Terry Johnson's schedule for evaluation of the potential reintroduction sites for the Mexican wolf.

Almost every day in late spring 1987, Arizona newspapers published stories about possible reintroduction of wolves and grizzlies, creating public concern. Speculation spread that legislators might prohibit reintroductions in Arizona, as had happened in Texas. To protect the AGFD's authorities, on June 9, 1987, Department Director Temple Reynolds wrote a letter to Frank Dunkle, then director of the USFWS, that said in part: "I believe that it is in the best interest of both the resource and the citizens of Arizona that the reintroduction of either species be put on the back burner for several years." The letter went on to stress the importance of public education about wolves to build support and ensure success for any future reintroduction program.

Despite this temporary setback, in August 1987, the Arizona Game and Fish (AGF) Commission adopted the Arizona 12-step procedure. The importance of the Arizona 12 step procedure to the Mexican wolf program and other endangered species programs cannot be overemphasized. The Arizona 12-step procedure established the steps to be followed during project implementation of any ESA species considered for reintroduction.

That same year, the AGFD proposed an objective survey of public attitudes about wolves in the Southwest. The USFWS and the USFS each offered $5,000 in matching funds for the AGFD to conduct the survey. In October 1987, Service Regional Director Michael Spear was widely quoted as fearing for the wolf recovery program, because the Department of the Army was no longer considering wolf reintroduction on White Sands Missile Range, the only site New Mexico had offered for evaluation; Texas had passed a law forbidding reintroduction of wolves; and Arizona had relegated their involvement to the "back burner."

On October 9, 1987, Spear was quoted in New Mexico newspapers as saying, "We have no [reintroduction] sites. The wolf reintroduction program, as of now, is terminated." Later he modified his position to say that alternate sites must be selected by September 20, 1988, or the program would be terminated.

Author and biologist David Brown, in a special column in the *Arizona Republic* on October 5, 1988, stated:

> The Game and Fish Department's nongame branch sought and received funding from the U.S. Fish and Wildlife Service and the Forest Service to survey attitudes toward releasing wolves in Arizona. The first phase of the survey was a random interview of 726 heads of households conducted by Behavior Research Center. The second phase was to be a mail questionnaire sent to both a random sample of the general public and to selected groups—conservationists, sportsmen's organizations, cattle growers, etc.
>
> The first phase was completed; the second phase was not. Almost as soon as the design of the questionnaire had been finalized, the Department was told to cancel the mailing. The Commission was afraid that even bringing up the subject of wolf reintroduction would irritate the ranching community and result in political consequences for the Department.
>
> Joe Lane, a rancher from Willcox, was House majority leader, and John Hays, a rancher from Yarnell, was the chair of the Senate Natural Resources Committee.

Although results of the telephone survey had revealed that 61 percent of those surveyed favored the return of the wolf, there was no organized citizen support for recovery in the state of Arizona. Organized opposition by the cattle industry and some hunters was strong. The AGFD shelved the second written phase of the survey. Unless the AGF Commission could be moved to reactivate the program that had been placed on the back burner, chances of any future freedom for the Mexican wolf were bleak.

For several months I began developing a plan on how to go about organizing a group of people to provide support for the AGFD's efforts on behalf of the Mexican wolf. The goal for the group would be the preservation and restoration of the Mexican wolf. I sent out a statement to several environmental organizations, announcing that a group was being formed to accomplish the goal of restoring the Mexican wolf.

The first mailing included background on Mexican wolves and the fact that their future was in great jeopardy, threatened with extinction. I did not try to load potential members down with the heavy ecological logic behind restoring the Mexican wolf to its former habitat. I did recommend that they read books like *The Wolf*, by David Mech (1970); *The Soul of the Wolf*, by Michael W. Fox (1980); and *The Wolf in the Southwest*, by David Brown (1984). The last one includes accurate documentation of the early existence of the Mexican wolf, and the tragic story of the extirpation program carried out by the federal government and its hired predator-killers. Brown provides a thorough discussion of the taxonomy and historical distribution of the Mexican wolf.

But what would I call this group? I came up with PAWS, which would stand for "Preserve Arizona's Wolves." I soon learned that there are probably a dozen animal rights groups throughout the United States called PAWS, so I made mine distinctive by the insertion of periods: "P.A.WS."

In May 1988, I wrote to Michael Spear at USFWS, informing him of my intent to form P.A.WS. and asking for status information on the Mexican wolf recovery program. I quote from his response of June 1988:

> The U.S. Fish and Wildlife Service started the Mexican Wolf Captive Breeding Program in 1979 with the capture of four wolves in Mexico. In 1982, the Mexican Wolf Recovery Plan was signed jointly by the United States and Mexico. States within the historic range of the subspecies (Arizona, New Mexico, Texas) were polled in 1986 to determine if suitable reintroduction sites existed, and White Sands Missile

Range was evaluated in 1987 as a possible reintroduction site. Three pairs of wolves were sent back to Mexico in 1987, and a fourth pair will be sent this year.

There are presently twenty-four Mexican wolves in the U.S. captive breeding program ... and six in Mexico. Four facilities in the U.S. have met criteria established by the Mexican Wolf Captive Breeding Committee (Arizona-Sonora Desert Museum, Wild Canid Survival and Research Center, Rio Grande Zoo, and Alamogordo Zoo).

Captive propagation is only one step in the recovery of this species, with establishment of two wild populations the goal to downlisting the subspecies to threatened. Cooperation with the State and land managing agency is required before reintroduction can begin. The Fish and Wildlife Service will continue to work with States and land managers in an effort to reintroduce Mexican wolves.

Years before my involvement with Mexican wolves, I had worked on public-land grazing issues. I had attended Allan Savory's Holistic Resource Management (HRM) schools and read his books, in which he stressed the importance of predators to the health of ungulate populations. I wrote Savory about my intended efforts on behalf of returning the Mexican wolf to the Southwest and won his total backing. This was to prove invaluable in the years ahead, because so many progressive ranchers in Arizona are disciples of HRM principles.

The initial announcement of P.A.WS.'s founding brought an unexpectedly strong supportive reaction from a large number of Arizonans, as well as wolf enthusiasts from around the United States. Within a month I found myself with a membership list of about 150. P.A.WS. had started to participate in fund-raising events, but I realized that it would be beneficial to encourage public funding for wolf recovery, and that it would be appropriate to have a trust fund administered by an organization better known than P.A.WS. into which such funds could be directed. I approached Terry Johnson about this, and he agreed to establish the Mexican Wolf Trust Fund, to be administered by the AGFD, where all donations would be dedicated to the Mexican wolf program.

If we were to move ahead in an effort to free the Mexican wolf, we needed to require the AGF Commission to reschedule the written public-attitude survey. I sent out a request to P.A.WS. members for letters to the AGF Commission, asking the Commission to proceed with the already funded written public-attitude survey. Several environmental publications picked up my request, giving it wide coverage. Much to the surprise and dismay of the Commission, this coverage generated more than one hundred letters. Early in 1989, the AGF Commission rescheduled the written public-attitude survey, and AGFD wildlife biologist Barry Spicer was assigned to finalize the questionnaire and conduct the survey.

During all of my early learning days on the Mexican wolf, one fact was driven home repeatedly. The public needs accurate information about wolves in order to make intelligent decisions about its future. Thus P.A.WS. must participate in a public education program. During the spring of 1989, I learned that the USFWS had contracted with a conservation educator, Dr. Carol Cochran, curator of education at the ASDM, to produce educational materials on the Mexican wolf. I called Cochran, introducing both myself and P.A.WS., and made an appointment to discuss the need for public wolf-education with her.

As soon as I encountered her striding across the sidewalk from the education buildings to the main court at ASDM to greet me, I could sense her forceful drive and energy. Back in the education meeting hall, this diminutive dynamo gave me a preview of the slide show she was producing under contract with the USFWS.

The show's text traced the history of the Mexican wolf, explaining factually why the wolf had been exterminated in the

Southwest. The text described wolf communication and behavior. It stated that perhaps the future for the Mexican wolf would be to remain in captivity, or perhaps the wolf's future might allow small populations in southwestern wilderness areas. The show encouraged the public to learn more about wolves, attend public meetings where decisions were being made about possible wolf recovery, and voice opinions as to what the future should hold for the Mexican wolf. Completion of the slide show was scheduled for late summer of 1989.

Cochran also gave me several copies of a descriptive brochure on the Mexican wolf, with text written by Norma Ames, that I might revise the text for use in Arizona. This was one of the first promotional pieces I published for our fledgling coalition, P.A.WS. As a result, I began corresponding with Ames to let her know about our organization and our intended use of the brochure. She became a valuable source of information.

As word got out about Cochran's slide show, requests for programs began. I was asked to make a presentation for the Arizona education group Arizona Association for Learning in and about the Environment (AALE) at their September 1989 three-day workshop, held in Prescott, Arizona.

Both the USFWS and AGFD had stressed the importance of public education to provide accurate information to the public, enabling people to make educated decisions about the wolf's future. I contacted Spear and asked when the slide show reviews would be completed and these educational materials released for use with the public. The reply to my inquiry was polite but indefinite.

I initiated another letter-writing campaign, this time to the nearly 250 interested P.A.WS. members, asking them to write requests to the USFWS to review and release the slide show. Again, responses were polite but indefinite. The slide show was being reviewed by staff in the USFWS Washington office, and they did not know how long that would take.

In mid-August, P.A.WS. participated in the Audubon Society's national convention in Tucson, where we had an information booth in the exhibit area. The keynote speaker for the convention was John Turner, then director for the USFWS. I confronted one of Turner's aides and related my dilemma over the delay in the slide show release.

"In September I'm to speak to a group of Arizona educators about the Mexican wolf. They expect to have the slide show presentation. How can I provide public education on the wolf if material being produced by the Service is not released?" I asked.

He promised to discuss the situation in Washington upon his return.

Within a week I received a call from Ken Russell, then deputy director under Spear, who said that the USFWS Washington staff had been apprised of the situation and had finished reviews and taken necessary papers to Manuel Lujan, then interior secretary, for the final approval signature. The Albuquerque office informed Cochran at ASDM to prepare copies of the slide show to be made available to the public.

One-half hour before I was to speak to educators at the September AALE conference, I was handed a copy of the finished slide show, "A Call for the Wild." I barely had a chance to review it before my presentation. The adult and children's slide shows became hallmarks of P.A.WS.'s education program and were eventually shown to hundreds of audiences of all ages.

Our Major Symposium

Man and nature must work hand in hand. The throwing out of balance of resources of nature throws out of balance also the lives of men.

—Franklin Delano Roosevelt, Message to Congress,
January 24, 1935

Results of the 1987 telephone survey revealed that much of the public didn't know that the Mexican wolf had once lived in the Southwest. P.A.WS. needed to create an event that would educate the public about wolves as well as put us on the map. Early in 1989, we decided to produce a symposium, even though neither I nor any of the members had any experience in staging such a meeting. We wanted the symposium to explore a variety of concerns about wolves. I put together a planning committee that included Carol Cochran, curator of education, and Peter Siminski, curator of mammals and birds, from the Arizona-Sonora Desert Museum (ASDM); Barry Spicer, nongame biologist from the Arizona Game and Fish Department (AGFD); and Tom Hulen, curator of education from the Pueblo Grande Museum. It was then spring 1989. We decided the symposium would take place in March 1990, and we called the event "Arizona Wolf Symposium '90."

It was our intent that people leaving the symposium would be more knowledgeable and accurately informed about wolves and issues related to them, and that, as a result, they would be better able to make decisions about the future role of wolves in the Southwest. Our symposium should inform, not inflame, the audience. We should present a unique experience where wildlife scientists and other educators, students, environmentalists, hunters, and ranchers who wanted to learn more about wolves could explore and discuss the subject together with an excellent roster of speakers to gain clearer insights. Our plans called for a forum to discuss varying perspectives of wolf recovery.

The results of the planning meeting were opened to further discussion at a Phoenix area P.A.WS. meeting, where responsibilities for various aspects of the symposium were assigned. I took on the overall planning as my full-time job.

Because P.A.WS. was so little known in the area, it seemed advisable to have a cosponsor for the event. The Arizona chapter of the Wildlife Society agreed to be that cosponsor in name only. I decided on Tempe's Arizona State University (ASU) Holiday Inn because its proximity to the campus gave it an academic connection. The symposium was set for March 23 and 24, 1990, and now all I had to do was produce it.

During the summer of 1989, I took a break from symposium planning to camp with my wolf-dogs at Riggs Flat Lake on Mount Graham. It was there that I first encountered Dennis Parker and his wife, Laura. They had stopped by to admire my wolf-dogs, and it wasn't long before the conversation turned to wolves. I told Dennis Parker about P.A.WS. and our plans to hold a symposium. He was intensely interested and proceeded to tell me why the U.S. Fish and Wildlife Service (USFWS) plans for Mexican wolf reintroduction were completely invalid. He insisted that there were still wolves coming over from Mexico and that that's where the emphasis should be, since all the wolves in the captive population were, he was certain, part dog.

He went on to tell me that he had a bachelor's degree in biology and had conducted years of fieldwork on Mexican wolf studies. He had found evidence of wolves along the old wolf runs in the Canelo Hills, including tracks and scat. He'd tried unsuccessfully to get the AGFD to fund his studies.

Later Terry Johnson confirmed that Parker had refused to reveal the sites for his reported evidence and therefore his requests for funding had been denied.

Although Parker was not able to convince the AGFD, P.A.WS., the Sierra Club, and Earth First! that his theories on the Mexican wolf were well founded, the Cochise Cattle Growers Association found his perspective as a biologist who opposed the USFWS plans for possible wolf recovery fit their cause very well. His viewpoint was later also taken up by several conservative legislators at the state capitol.

During this period our symposium-planning committee had established objectives. I wanted the best representatives from the red wolf program and the northern Rocky Mountain wolf program as well as spokespeople for the fledgling Mexican wolf recovery program. In addition to invited speakers, we sent out a call for papers for others who might like to speak at our event.

Our list of invited speakers read like a who's who of wolfdom, including such names as Roy McBride, rancher and trapper from Texas; Julio Carrera, parks director of Mexico; Warren Parker, recovery coordinator of the red wolf program; Steve Fritts, recovery coordinator for the northern Rocky Mountain wolf project; and David Brown, author and wildlife biologist. I invited Hank Fischer, northwest representative for Defenders of Wildlife, as one of the forum speakers, and for balance, but against the advice of my planning committee, I invited Dennis Parker to participate.

Much to my surprise, nearly all of those invited agreed to come. P.A.WS. had agreed to pay all travel and lodging expenses for out-of-state speakers. My heart was set on having Dr. L. David Mech (pronounced "meech"), recognized throughout the world as the leading authority on wolf behavior, as the keynote speaker. Early attempts to gain his acceptance failed. Friendly persuasion from my friend Deborah Warrick, then editor of the magazine *Wolves and Related Canids,* who had once worked for Mech in Minnesota, snagged him.

Our only problem now was where to find the money. Although the speakers' acceptances were encouraging, P.A.WS. was not yet financially capable of covering their expenses or the many other costs involved with this undertaking. At a minimum we needed $10,000.

Negative—sometimes harshly negative—responses to thirty grant applications brought reality crashing down around me. Some foundations would not even consider our grant proposal because we were not an IRS-qualified 501 (c) (3) organization. Lack of this classification meant that their gift would not be tax deductible. I learned that I'd better move on this 501 (c) (3) thing soon. Several rejections stated that the subject of the symposium was not compatible with their foundations' objectives. The harsh reality I had to accept was that these foundations were exhibiting their aversion to an educational program that focused on wolves.

My twenty-eight years of experience in electronics at Honeywell had immersed me in a world of polarization, where zeros and ones make up binary bits that influence the polarization of the magnetic flux and make the computers do their work. In the multitude of combinations that these binary bits find themselves, a single zero or one out of place could crash an entire computer system. Solving these problems was maddening and often stressful, but nothing in my professional career had prepared me for the task of resolving the formidable antipathy that many otherwise intelligent people harbored against wolves. I was baffled as to how to influence the polarization that separated the wolf advocates from the wolf haters.

Even the national Wildlife Society turned down my proposal

after months of my providing much in-depth information and subsequent back-and-forth correspondence. This was a real blow because their Arizona Wildlife Society had agreed to cosponsor the event and had contributed a modest amount. Predictable environmental groups such as the Sierra Club and Audubon Society provided limited grants, but the total was not near what was needed. Where could I turn for help?

Defenders of Wildlife Southwest Representative Steve Johnson had been highly supportive of my efforts with P.A.WS. He recognized the need for widespread wolf education and told me that Defenders would cover expenses for Hank Fischer. Johnson directed me to Dan Bates, who had regularly supported Defenders. Dan and his mother, Mary Bates, headed the AGRO Land and Cattle Company, Inc., and Johnson recommended I send them a proposal describing our program with a request for funding. He, in turn, would contact them personally about the worthiness of the symposium. Their response was a generous $2,000 grant.

Several other local small groups came through with small grants, but even when combined with the other pledges, our total was only $6,000, far less than our Spartan budget of $10,000.

I discussed our financial crisis with Terry Johnson. He said he'd try to get funding through the AGFD for this educational program. He made a formal request to the department director, Duane Shroufe, but was turned down.

"I think it would be a good idea if you wrote Duane a letter," Johnson advised.

I wrote to Duane Shroufe, explaining our need and requesting a grant of $1,000. Several weeks later, Johnson related Shroufe's response to my letter. "He said that while he sees the value of such a conference, he believes that for the Department to openly sponsor anything so obviously involved with the wolf would be too proactive. He did agree that Department staff can continue to lend support." The Department also agreed to supply and staff all audio-visual equipment.

Shroufe's refusal to help fund our educational symposium brought on tears, but I was determined to find funding somewhere.

P.A.WS. participated in the Tempe Arts Festival, where we took in about $1,000 from the sale of T-shirts I had purchased at my own expense. We funneled most of the proceeds back into the purchase of additional T-shirts and posters to sell at the symposium. Besides funding speakers' travel and lodging expenses, we faced additional up-front expenses, such as printing the programs and the proceedings that we wanted to distribute at the gathering.

In sheer desperation, I called Ken Russell, one of the USFWS deputy assistant regional directors, in Albuquerque.

"Ken, we've got all these great speakers committed to speak at our symposium and not enough money to bring them here. I've sent out thirty grant proposals and still we've raised only $6,000. Nobody wants to openly support wolves." At this point I had to control myself to keep from crying over the phone. "Even with our lean budget we can't pull this off for less than $10,000. How's it going to look when I have to tell David Mech, Warren Parker, and Steve Fritts that we've canceled the symposium because we can't afford to fly them here?"

Russell understood my dilemma. "I see your problem," he stated. "I'll get back to you soon."

A week later Russell called back from Albuquerque. "The Service will pick up all expenses of those of your speakers who are Fish and Wildlife employees because it would be within standard Service policy for payment of employee travel expenses," he announced. Because the USFWS had not yet fully committed to Mexican wolf reintroduction, he asked that they not be listed as a sponsor on our program.

I was overjoyed. This support and an unexpected boost from the Albuquerque regional Forest Service put us over the top. I'd been discussing my financial crisis with Leon Fisher, Forest Service Region 3 biologist. Now that the lead agency on endangered species programs, the USFWS, had agreed to lend its support, the Forest Service provided additional financial assistance.

Arizona Wolf Symposium '90 was now a go.

In the meantime, committees were moving along with plans for registration and publications. We needed convincing press materials for the news media; under guidance from a Sierra Club pamphlet on press kits, we produced kits containing inserts, including background information on wolves, myths and misconceptions, questions and answers on wolves, and photographs. AGFD's Barry Spicer had become a valuable advisor on many phases of symposium preparation, and he agreed to write the much needed "Selected Chronology on Wolves with Focus on the Mexican Wolf."

Spicer was already working long hours on the written public-attitude survey, the results of which he'd be presenting at the symposium. He sent out a comprehensive questionnaire to a cross-section of Arizona's citizens, including Department employees, members of the Arizona Cattle Growers Association (ACGA), hunters, members of Defenders of Wildlife, rural Arizona households, and urban Arizona households. At the eleventh hour, Sandy Eastlake, executive vice president of the ACGA, withdrew the group's participation in the survey, claiming that the questionnaire was flawed. Eastlake made this decision without consulting with other ACGA officials, and Terry Johnson later told me, "Phil Clifton and other members of their board of directors were unaware that ACGA had been withdrawn from the survey. They told me that it would have been in their best interests to have had their opinions represented."

As the date for Arizona Wolf Symposium '90 drew nearer,

Phoenix P.A.WS. member Tom Hulen was doing a fine job preparing copies of the symposium speakers' talks for our proceedings. Another member, Terri Volk, was effectively handling all symposium registrations. Staff at the Tempe Holiday Inn was most accommodating in planning arrangements for meal and snack menus and with making room reservations.

We prepared fliers announcing the event and distributed them throughout the Phoenix area. I distributed press kits to about forty members of the press and members of the television media a few weeks before the March event. Staff from the AGFD, assisted by P.A.WS. volunteer Jerry Palmer, set up audiovisual equipment in the large conference room. An ASU student volunteered to videotape the entire program as a project for one of her media production classes.

Longtime friend, nationally known artist, and strong supporter of wilderness and wildlife Anne Coe designed a whimsical poster celebrating Arizona Wolf Symposium '90. Copies of this incredible contribution would be offered for sale with wolf T-shirts during the symposium.

As the symposium opened the evening of Friday, March 23, we were overwhelmed by many people who had not registered. This delayed the start of the evening session. Don Henry, President of the ASU chapter of the Wildlife Society, joined me in welcoming attendees. Michael Phillips, then project leader on the red wolf program, talked on that project's success, and Jack Laufer, biologist from Wolf Haven International, reported on surveying the return of wolves from Canada into Washington. These were among five fine papers presented during the Friday evening session.

On Saturday morning, we were besieged by an even larger crowd of nonregistered participants and had to postpone some registrations until the mid-morning break in order to get under way at a reasonable time. The crowd of more than four hundred people filled the conference hall to overflowing. Not only were wolf advocates present, but we had several ranchers, officers of the ACGA, Animal Damage Control (ADC) staff, and members of Earth First!, Sierra Club, and other environmental and wildlife groups.

Tom Hulen and Mike Seidman, lead keeper from the Phoenix Zoo, started this session by presenting history and myths. Roy McBride horrified yet fascinated the diverse group as he told how he'd trapped Mexican wolves for the federal wolf extermination program and later was hired to capture a few wolves in Mexico to start the captive-breeding program.

Terry Johnson followed up with a discussion of Mexican wolf habitat preferences. Bud Weiser, curator of mammals for the Alamogordo Zoo, told us there were now thirty-nine Mexican wolves held at nine facilities in the United States and Mexico. Julio Carrera described locations in Mexico where small populations of Mexican wolves might yet survive.

To further dispel existing myths about wolves, David Brown told about his firsthand experiences with wolves in Italy and Spain. He posed the question, "If wolves can survive in populated areas of Italy and Spain, why can't they live in our southwestern wilderness?" Then Barry Spicer gave us the first official results from the written public-attitude survey he had just completed. He distributed preliminary copies of the survey that showed heavy support for the Mexican wolf reintroduction but indicated a lack of accurate information about wolf behavior among those surveyed.

The survey pointed out the critical need for better public education programs on wolves. Spicer's presentation was followed by that of Carol Cochran, who presented her slide show "A Call for the Wild," and Lorna Taylor, a Tucson teacher, who described her elementary school wolf curriculum.

Larry Allen, range coordinator for the Coronado National Forest, covered habitat management for Mexican wolves, and Ken Russell discussed administrative responsibilities. Warren

P.A.WS. used wolf photos and other materials to inform the symposium audience about the history of early captive Mexican wolves. Photo by Russell Lampertz. Courtesy of U.S. Fish and Wildlife Service.

David Mech gave the symposium keynote speech. Photo by Carol Osman Brown.

Parker, Steve Fritts, and Peter Siminski described current wolf recovery programs. Dennis Parker challenged Siminski's statements by suggesting that the Mexican wolves in captivity were all hybrid dogs.

David Mech captivated the audience with his keynote speech and slides on his experiences with the white wolves of Ellesmere Island. His authentic up-close pictures of wolves, showing their soul-searching glances, mischievous gestures, affectionate posturing, and prey interaction held everyone spellbound during his memorable presentation.

The final event was a forum expressing differing perspectives on wolf recovery. Forum members were Allan Savory, outspoken advocate for the coexistence of cattle and predators;

Dennis Parker; Phil Clifton, eastern Arizona rancher and member of the board of directors of the ACGA; Hank Fischer; and Ace Peterson, sportsman and executive in the Arizona Wildlife Federation (AWF).

Savory stressed the wolf's beneficial attributes in promoting herding among grazing animals and by culling unhealthy members of ungulate populations. Parker spoke of the historical territory of the Mexican wolf and the need to study existing populations of wolves in Mexico. Clifton emphasized ranchers' concerns about the problems that returning the wolf would have on domestic animals and his belief that the safe approach would be no reintroduction of the wolf. Hank Fischer discussed Defenders' wolf compensation program, which offered "supply-side" environmentalism as a means of resolving ranchers' losses from depredation. Peterson told the audience that most sportsmen would find that the return of the wolf would bring wildness to the land and wilderness adventure to their hunting experience. The audience held a wide diversity of opinions on the five forum talks, reflected in provocative questions and comments ranging from outright opposition to cattle grazing to the drastic effects wolves would have on cattle-grazing operations. The forum members defended their individual perspectives on wolf reintroduction, offering no consensus but a hope that working toward common goals might resolve the problems that existed between those favoring and those opposed to Mexican wolf reintroduction.

Our wolf symposium was a howling success. We'd opened a hospitality room for speakers and the press both nights following the sessions, and this provided excellent opportunities for networking among representative key players in the world of wolves. Ken Russell commented to me, "The Mexican wolf recovery program is not going to take any giant steps but will proceed by little increments. Your symposium constituted a bunch of little increments."

Many local press writers covered the symposium. Despite the fact that the diverse audience did not display any animosity, the press could not resist running headlines proclaiming "Repopulation of Gray Wolf Spurs Howls of Controversy," and "Fight Looms around Reintroduction of Gray Wolf." Their articles implied open controversy at the symposium, which had never occurred. David Brown reported it accurately in his article "Wolves Need Human Allies to Make Restoration Successful," which appeared in the April 23, 1990, issue of *High Country News,* noting that everyone was on their best behavior and no arguments ensued.

P.A.WS. did so well financially at Arizona Wolf Symposium '90, from both the abundance of registration fees and many T-shirt and poster sales, that we cleared about $5,000. We planned to donate a large portion of this to the already established Mexican Wolf Trust Fund, administered by the AGFD, to be used in their educational and outreach efforts. The rest would be used for our educational needs and for future fund-raising merchandise.

At about the same time, the Mexican Wolf Coalition of New Mexico, along with the Wolf Action Group (WAG) and other New Mexico wolf advocates, were becoming increasingly frustrated over the continued curtailment of the Mexican wolf reintroduction process. They were out of patience with the inaction of the USFWS and the U.S. Army, who had withdrawn permission for wolves to be reintroduced on the White Sands Missile Base. After Michael Spear's unfortunate statement that the Mexican wolf reintroduction program was, in effect, terminated, the whole recovery program was at a standstill. The Mexican Wolf Captive-Breeding Program was stalled, and program staff made no attempt to encourage producing any more pups as long as there were inadequate facilities for housing them. Prospects for Mexican wolf reintroduction were indeed grim.

WAG collected about fifteen thousand signatures on petitions favoring reintroduction of the wolf into White Sands, and they glued the petitions together into a long streamer. The advocates marched to the Service's offices with the petition and a letter of intent to file a lawsuit against both the USFWS and the U.S. Army and staged a meaningful demonstration covered by the media. They presented Spear the mile-long petition and the letter. Grove Burnett, director of the Western Environmental Law Center, was the attorney for the plaintiffs. The lawsuit claimed both the USFWS and the U.S. Army were in violation of the ESA for curtailing the Mexican wolf recovery program.

P.A.WS. was asked to join this effort, but we declined. We believed that the USFWS had made positive progress by supporting our educational symposium, and for us to join a lawsuit against them would be inappropriate.

Soon after Arizona Wolf Symposium '90, the New Mexico wolf advocates filed their lawsuit against the USFWS and the U.S. Army. The tireless effort put forth by these wolf advocates jarred both the Service and the army into reversing their positions on Mexican wolf reintroduction. Their efforts created a major turning point for Mexican wolves.

P.A.WS. Takes Positive Action

We need a process for resolving endangered species issues that brings people together instead of dividing them.
—Hank Fischer, *Wolf Wars*

Two major needs arose from the symposium. One was the need for public education that would provide accurate information about wolves. The other, pointed out to me by Ken Russell of the U.S. Fish and Wildlife Service (USFWS), was the need to establish a compensation fund for Mexican wolf depredation, even though actual reintroduction was years away.

Kerry Baldwin, education branch chief for the Arizona Game and Fish Department (AGFD), provided excellent guidance in setting up a workshop to instruct potential educators. He had long promoted use of Project WILD programs, environmental and conservation programs for teachers. Baldwin helped me to outline a simple course of instruction for classroom presentations that would include use of the "A Call for the Wild" slide show and stress important features about wolf behavior and communication.

I conducted two all-day workshops for about fifteen P.A.WS. members. I hoped that by training others we could spread the word faster, but most of those who attended worked Monday through Friday, when the schools needed the programs. Melinda Butler, a homemaker, provided many weekday programs for the public libraries, and other members provided educational programs in the Flagstaff area. For several years, I visited classrooms and spoke at various adult meetings around Arizona once or twice a week, providing educational programs about wolves. Over the years of P.A.WS.'s existence, we were involved in at least five hundred educational or public outreach events.

Russell told me that it would help his contacts with livestock groups if our private wolf advocate group were to establish a Mexican wolf compensation fund to cover future livestock depredation caused by Mexican wolves. Wildlife is held in public trust, but the federal and state agencies that administer protective programs for wildlife cannot afford to administer depredation funds covering damages from the activities of wildlife. Mexican wolf advocates could put their money where their mouths were by offering livestock depredation compensation.

I opened a new bank account called "Mexican Wolf Compensation Fund" and deposited $1,000 into it. Susan Larson, then president of the Mexican Wolf Coalition of New Mexico, did the same. So a compensation fund now existed, although it was obvious that $2,000 would not be adequate to ensure coverage for future wolf depredation.

At that time, the Mexican wolf was a low priority issue with Defenders of Wildlife, and it was not an issue to which Steve Johnson had been assigned. In late 1989, Defenders closed their Southwest office and terminated Johnson's employment. Defenders had told him that they no longer needed representation in this region. Johnson quickly established an ecological consulting service, Native Ecosystems, and has remained active in many wildlife projects.

With Johnson gone from Defenders, I began to obtain more and more advice from Hank Fischer, Defenders's northern Rocky Mountain representative in Missoula, Montana. I asked Fischer if he thought Defenders would expand their compensation fund to include Mexican wolves. He believed it ought to be done, but staff in Defenders's Washington office, then under President Ruppert Cutler, were focusing on translocating gray wolves from

Canada to Yellowstone and were not interested in the Mexican wolf. Fischer promised to promote the idea because biologically, the Mexican wolf, on the brink of extinction, was the most endangered subspecies of wolf in the world.

Larry Allen, range coordinator for the Coronado National Forest, offered me a tour of the former wolf habitat in southeastern Arizona. I felt this was too valuable not to share with others. In fall 1991, I invited Terry Johnson and Russell who, in turn, invited a few other Game and Fish, Fish and Wildlife Service, and Forest Service staff to what would be a two-day tour. A friend of mine, Rob MacNeil of Hereford, Arizona, offered his home as our overnight headquarters. During those two days, we viewed the old wolf runs and heard stories from Allen that ranchers had related of earlier wolf sightings. We drove through former wolf country in the Huachucas, San Rafael Valley, and Patagonia Mountains the first day, and then east on the second day to the Peloncillo Mountains over into the Gray Ranch country of New Mexico.

As we toured these rolling hills and wide valleys, Johnson told me that the AGFD biologists had narrowed the list of fifteen possible reintroduction sites down to four potential sites: the Patagonia/Atascosa Mountains, the Chiricahua Mountains and adjacent lands, the Galiuro/Pinaleno Mountains, and the Blue Range Area in the White Mountains. He said that at the August Arizona Game and Fish (AGF) Commission meeting, he was going to request that the Commission approve funding to submit a proposal to the USFWS for evaluation of these four sites.

Subsequently, P.A.WS. members generated many letters to the AGF Commission, asking for their approval of Johnson's request. At the August meeting where the request was approved, I presented AGFD Director Duane Shroufe with a check for $3,000, on behalf of P.A.WS., for deposit into the Mexican Wolf Trust Fund.

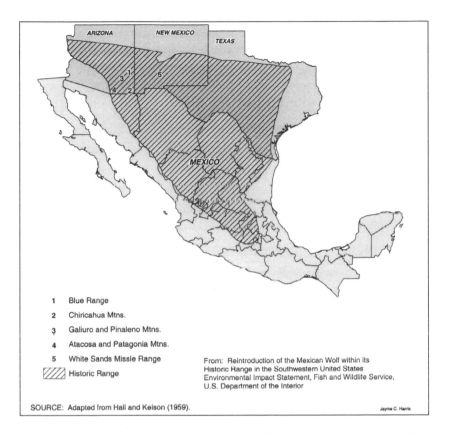

1   Blue Range
2   Chiricahua Mtns.
3   Galiuro and Pinaleno Mtns.
4   Atacosa and Patagonia Mtns.
5   White Sands Missle Range

///// Historic Range

From: Reintroduction of the Mexican Wolf within its Historic Range in the Southwestern United States Environmental Impact Statement, Fish and Wildlife Service, U.S. Department of the Interior

SOURCE: Adapted from Hall and Kelson (1959).   Jayme C. Harris

Approximate historic range of the Mexican gray wolf, indicating the five candidate areas for releasing wolves.

One of the members of the AGF Commission was Tom Woods, former executive vice president and chief operating officer of Arizona Public Service. Tom served on the AGF Commission from 1986 until 1992. Tom remained neutral about the Mexican wolf reintroduction program until about 1991. Then, after studying the Mexican Wolf Recovery Plan, he became thoroughly convinced that the wolf should be returned to its rightful habitat. Tom steered other Commission members toward support of Mexican wolf recovery.

P.A.WS. generated letters to Congress asking for additional funding for the USFWS Mexican wolf recovery program. Because of an interagency agreement, originating in Section 6 of the ESA, certain amounts of this funding from the Service could trickle down to the AGFD for their use in endangered species programs. Using these funds, Terry Johnson assigned two AGFD biologists, Debbie Noel and Laurie Ward, the task of studying the four potential reintroduction sites in Arizona and preparing a report on their conclusions.

Following the filing of the New Mexico wolf advocates' lawsuit, USFWS Region 2 Director Michael Spear reversed his earlier decision to terminate the Mexican wolf recovery program. A new general appointed to the White Sands Missile Range reversed the army's earlier refusal to allow the reintroduction of Mexican wolves to the wild mountainous lands east of the proving grounds. Spear made a statement to the press that he hoped to see Mexican wolves released in late 1992. The Mexican wolf captive population at that time was only forty-four.

Late in 1990, Spear appointed David Parsons, who had previously been on the Albuquerque field staff, to be the Mexican wolf recovery coordinator. Parsons earned his bachelor's degree in fisheries and wildlife biology in 1969 from Iowa State University and his master's degree in wildlife biology in 1975 from Oregon State University. This was his first experience with a wolf recovery effort. Parsons immediately started working on a status report and a funding proposal.

Parsons wanted to learn how the public would react to Mexican wolf recovery and scheduled a series of scoping meetings during February 1991, in Arizona and New Mexico, to receive comments. Sonny Lopez of the *Las Cruces Journal* described a Monday Las Cruces, New Mexico, meeting as a "heckling match" where "supporters of the Mexican gray wolf and ranchers traded howls and cackles during a five-hour public comment meeting that ended early Tuesday." At the Tucson meeting, held on February 27, 1991, the messages Parsons received from both sides of the issue were loud and clear. P.A.WS. members along with representatives from Sierra Club, Earth First!, and other advocate groups testified strongly in favor of el lobo's return. Wolf haters delivered shrill blasts of opposition, claiming that there was no longer any suitable habitat for the wolf in the Southwest. Later reports of the meeting revealed that 70 percent of the testimony favored the wolf's return.

Ever since the 1990 symposium, I had been working on the Internal Revenue Service's complicated application forms for the coveted 501 (c) (3) nonprofit status. Part of the requirements called for a board of directors. I quickly formed one, composed of Carol Cochran and Peter Siminski, from the Arizona-Sonora Desert Museum (ASDM); Tom Hulen, from the Pueblo Grande Museum; Terri Volk, keeper at the Phoenix Zoo; and Steve Johnson, from Native Ecosystems. I appointed myself executive director of the board. Finally, in April 1991, we received our form letter of acceptance from the IRS. This classification made P.A.WS. eligible for nonprofit bulk mail rates at the post office and also made possible our participation in events that included only official nonprofit organizations.

During this period, I ran up large phone bills getting advice from Defenders's Hank Fischer in Missoula, Montana. He was working full time on getting wolves back into Yellowstone National Park. A few environmental groups used wolf reintroduction as a front for their real agenda to remove cattle grazing from public lands. They even created bumper stickers proclaiming "WOLVES! NOT COWS." This approach was not shared by Defenders of Wildlife or P.A.WS. I shared Fischer's belief that any reintroduction program without cooperation from the livestock industry would not long be successful. While it was clear that the cattle people might never really accept the need for wolves for ecological reasons, certain incentives could make the wolves' presence more palatable.

Such an incentive was Defenders's wolf compensation fund, initiated by Fischer. Defenders had the facilities for administering such a fund much more effectively than a small grassroots group like P.A.WS. It was imperative that their Washington staff become convinced to include the Mexican wolf in their compensation fund's coverage. When Rodger Schlickeisen took over the job of Defenders president, Fischer was able to convince him and the board of directors to support the endangered Mexican wolf.

In March 1991, in Tempe, Arizona, Fischer held a press conference announcing that Defenders would establish a compensation fund for Mexican wolves. P.A.WS. kicked off the fund by contributing our compensation fund, now grown to $3,000; the Mexican Wolf Coalition of New Mexico later contributed $1,000 from their account. This fund was later combined into Defenders's wolf compensation fund and administered as a trust.

About this time, Craig Miller, a P.A.WS. member who lived in Tempe and worked as a clerk for Recreation Equipment Incorporated, demonstrated interest in P.A.WS.'s activities. Craig had completed two years toward his bachelor's degree in outdoor recreation at the University of Nebraska before moving to Arizona. He told me he wanted to land a job with a national conservation organization and asked me to help him meet people in a position to assist him with his goal. Because of his apparent enthusiasm for a wildlife career, I made possible for Craig a scholarship to attend one of Allan Savory's HRM schools, where he met many progressive ranchers and wildlife specialists. I advised him to obtain his bachelor's degree before expecting any national conservation organization to offer him a job. In 1991, he moved to Flagstaff and enrolled at Northern Arizona University to complete his undergraduate studies.

It was becoming apparent that while Hank Fischer had been most helpful, we needed a Defenders representative in the Southwest. I believed that with sufficient training, Craig Miller might qualify for this position once he had completed his undergraduate work at Northern Arizona University. I began corresponding with Rodger Schlickeisen, requesting that Defenders consider Miller as a future employee.

In May 1991, Parsons received an important letter from David Mech, who chaired the International Union for Conservation of Nature's Wolf Specialist Group. This letter stated:

> This is to confirm that the Wolf Specialist Group considers Mexican wolf recovery to be the highest priority need for wolf conservation the world over. Although our group has no funding, we do meet annually to decide which international projects to recommend for funding, and for the past two years have recognized the strong need of the Mexican wolf. The recent genetics research indicating that Mexican wolves possess an apparently unique mitochondrial DNA haplotype certainly underscores our priority ranking for this work.

Parsons made copies of this letter available to Mexican wolf advocates, who welcomed the information. Mech's message was used widely in public presentations, press conferences, and congressional lobbying.

In February 1991, the Arizona Wool Producers had sent a memo directed to Parsons in which they listed conditions under which they would not oppose reintroduction of the Mexican wolf. The conditions included designation of the subspecies as nonessential experimental; interdepartmental cooperation between the U.S. Department of the Interior (USDI), U.S. Department of Agriculture (USDA), USFWS, and Animal Damage Control (ADC); and assurance that they would be provided updates on the process. This was welcome news, but there were few sheep-grazing allotments in any of the areas being considered for wolf reintroduction. More essential was cooperation from the Arizona Cattle Growers Association (ACGA).

Sandy Eastlake, executive vice president of the ACGA, granted permission for Fischer and me to speak at their August 1991 annual convention. Fischer agreed to leave cool Montana and come to the hot summer desert to speak with me at the ACGA convention in Tucson. We intended to convince their game committee to change their long-standing resolution opposing any form of Mexican wolf reintroduction to a more moderate stance.

I spoke briefly before introducing Fischer and told the committee that the majority of citizens wanted to see the Mexican wolves return, and the process was under way. I encouraged them to at least study the USFWS proposals for Mexican wolf reintroduction. I well remember Fischer's strident statement to the cattle growers. "You can either say 'Hell no—no wolves no way' and remove yourselves from the ball game, or you can have a voice in the process and review and comment on the forthcoming Arizona Game and Fish and Fish and Wildlife documents." He went on to say that when wolves came into Montana in 1987, the ranchers thought it meant the end of ranching. "When the first steer was killed, Defenders came out with their compensation fund. The rancher was reimbursed. There's only been a few livestock lost since then, and in each case the ranchers were given the market value for their losses." Fischer told the cattle growers that Montana folks were growing used to the idea of wolves' presence and no longer got very excited when more wolves migrated across from Canada. He assured the cattle growers that Defenders stood behind the wolf compensation fund. "Ten years from now, Arizona people will probably wonder what all the fuss was about."

On Sunday, after our Friday meeting with the cattle growers, I called a rancher friend, Diana Kessler, who had attended the convention. She and her husband, Alan, were active in the ACGA, and I thought she might know what effect Fischer's and my presentation may have had.

To my amazement, Kessler told me that the committee had come up with a resolution that reversed their former stand and established criteria they believed any wolf reintroduction program should meet. Later, from the ACGA's September–October 1991 *Cattlelog* magazine, I learned that their new resolution read in part, "The Arizona Cattle Growers members need a healthy and productive environment, and have supported policies to that end. We recognize the important role of predators in maintaining a healthy and productive environment and support the study of reintroduction. . . ."

The resolution went on to list seven conditions, including the following:

> The introduced animals must come from a pure gene pool.
>
> Any wolves released must be designated as an experimental population, which is non-essential to the survival of the species as defined in the Endangered Species Act.
>
> There will be interdepartmental cooperation between the U.S. Fish and Wildlife Service and the U.S. Department of Agriculture . . . to eliminate those animals that are engaged in predation on livestock and capture and return straying animals to the recovery area with the Fish and Wildlife Service covering the costs.
>
> There will be a fully and continually funded reimbursement program for livestock losses from wolf predation.

Spear told me that when he heard the news in Albuquerque that the Arizona cattle growers had had a change of heart, he nearly fell off his chair. He exclaimed, "This was indeed a major and unprecedented breakthrough."

P.A.WS. had repeatedly held letter-writing campaigns to congressional leaders in Washington, seeking an increase in the Interior Appropriations Subcommittee's funding for the

Mexican wolf. Each time our requests were denied. Using the May 1991 Mech letter, we initiated another letter drive, this time directing letters to President George Bush, asking him to include an increase in his fiscal year '93 budget, to be published in 1992.

During the fall of 1991, Laurie Ward and Debbie Noel, the AGFD biologists assigned to study the four potential wolf reintroduction sites, gave status reports to Phoenix P.A.WS. members. They explained their research process and the mapping and geological procedures they followed together with on-site inspection of the sites. They said that having to spend time on other AGFD priorities had somewhat delayed their progress.

I was disturbed by the reported delays and wrote a letter to Terry Johnson expressing my dismay over hearing that other Department priorities had forced the two biologists to delay the site studies. I indicated that the wolf project should have top priority among Department nongame projects. I backed up my concerns by sending a copy of the letter to AGFD Director Duane Shroufe.

Terry Johnson replied that my fears were possibly unnecessary and went on to explain the Department schedule for completion and review of the site studies. He wrote: "Both Debbie and Laurie are very hard workers and their expertise and energies are invaluable in many areas of our overall program. The wolf project is one of the more important areas, but from my perspective it is neither the only project nor the most important project that warrants their attention." Johnson's stern but kind admonishment of my inappropriate criticism made me recognize that I was not in a position to determine AGFD policies, priorities, or timelines.

The USFWS decided that despite the favorable comments they had received during the comment period, existing opposition was fierce enough to warrant preparing a full-fledged

Environmental Impact Statement (EIS) rather than just an environmental assessment for the proposed Mexican wolf reintroduction. Many wolf sightings were being reported along the Mexican border. Some of the reports originated from the opposition as a bogus attempt intended to preclude reintroduction.

Parsons published a timeline showing the EIS preparation beginning in 1992, with publication of a draft EIS in January 1993, and a final version to be completed by September 1993. Parsons dissolved the original Mexican wolf recovery team and appointed a new one late in 1991. He appointed himself team leader and chose the other members: Larry Allen, range coordinator from the Coronado National Forest; Terry Johnson, nongame chief from the AGFD; Jose Ma. Reyes Gomez from SEDUE, an environmental and conservation group in Mexico; and Sartor Williams III, from the New Mexico Department of Game and Fish. As consultants, Parsons named Warren Parker, retired USFWS red wolf recovery coordinator; Steve Fritts, USFWS Rocky Mountain wolf recovery coordinator; and Peter Siminski, curator of mammals and birds from ASDM.

This team decided that any reintroduction of Mexican wolves would be done using the ESA's nonessential-experimental classification. This classification had been used in the Yellowstone/Idaho EIS and provided biologists more flexibility in wolf management than the rigid full protection.

Near the end of 1991, Parsons and Siminski traveled to Mexico to collect blood samples from all of Mexico's Mexican wolf facilities. These would be added to already gathered blood samples of U.S. captive Mexican wolves for extensive DNA forensic testing by Dr. Robert Wayne of UCLA and the USFWS forensic laboratories in Oregon. In addition, the Mexican Wolf Recovery Team decided that the Ghost Ranch and Mexico's Aragon lineages of Mexican wolves would be tested as to whether or not they could be certified as pure wolves.

On March 14, 1992, Terry Johnson presented the draft

*Summary of Information on Four Potential Mexican Wolf Reintro-
duction Areas in Arizona* to the AGF Commission, during a public meeting in Tucson. The report, compiled with Debbie Noel
and Laurie Ward, described all four potential reintroduction
areas and prioritized them as to suitability as Mexican wolf
habitat. The White Mountains' Blue Range Area ranked first,
with the Patagonia/Atascosa Mountains ranking a close second.

This presentation initiated a sixty-day public comment period during which written comments were accepted on the document. The Department scheduled forty-one public meetings
and seventy-three individual presentations throughout the state
where concerned people could ask questions and clarify information prior to submitting their written comments. One of
these meetings, held in Alpine, Arizona, drew howls of protest
when it was learned that the Blue Range Area was first on the
potential list for Mexican wolf reintroduction.

About this time, the Arizona Wildlife Federation (AWF) asked
me to write an in-depth editorial for their *Arizona Wildlife News*
on why the Mexican wolf should be returned. My editorial,
published in January 1992, pointed out our moral responsibility to conserve all species and our mistake in removing the
wolf from the Southwest. It went on to describe efforts of the
USFWS and AGFD to restore the Mexican wolf to its historical
habitat, and how P.A.WS. was supporting their efforts.

I was unprepared for Dennis Parker's two-page response
in the February issue of the AWF newspaper. He lambasted
P.A.WS.'s motives, saying that we were less concerned about the
well-being of the Mexican wolf than the opportunity that this
animal had provided us to further our agenda and to increase
donations. Parker's diatribe also contained several errors concerning the USFWS process, potential Mexican wolf habitat,
and genetic viability of the Mexican wolves in the captive-
breeding program.

I wrote a brief but polite answer that appeared in the March issue, acknowledging Parker's years of study of the Mexican wolf but correcting the errors in his February response to my editorial.

This was followed in April by a full-page letter from Parker in the *Arizona Wildlife News,* in which he raked me over the coals for not being accountable to the people of Arizona, saying I provided deceptive and erroneous information on the Mexican wolf. He concluded with "perhaps Ms. Holaday will explain to all of us why it is that she has so blatantly misrepresented, and continues to misrepresent, all that she alleges to champion."

I had no intention of continuing this counter-productive debate with Parker. I sent copies of the series of *Arizona Wildlife News* articles to Spear at USFWS, to ensure that my statements pertaining to the recovery project were accurate. Spear's response was a complete invalidation of Parker's accusations and inaccurate claims. He concluded with "It has been my experience that Preserve Arizona's Wolves (P.A.WS.) has consistently exhibited the highest standards of integrity and honesty with regard to the presentation and dissemination of factual information. I also appreciate your respect for those whose views may differ from yours. P.A.WS.'s efforts in support of the Mexican wolf recovery program are greatly appreciated."

In May 1992, I attempted to get the Alpine District of the Forest Service to arrange a public meeting at which I would present the USFWS-sponsored slide show "A Call for the Wild." Don Hoffman of the Alpine District Forest Service office told me that the Forest Service would not sponsor such a meeting because it might give the appearance that they favored Mexican wolf reintroduction. I found it hard to believe that after the USFWS had officially announced that they were implementing the Mexican wolf recovery program, the U.S. Forest Service (USFS) would not cooperate with an educational program to provide accurate information about wolves to the public. The White Mountain Conservation League, an environmental group Hoffman and his wife had founded some years before, provided arrangements for the meeting, which was well attended.

My wolf-dogs accompanied me on this trip, and following the presentation, we camped a few days at Luna Lake. One rainy evening, Luke stumbled out of my camper on his way to relieve himself and completely collapsed. He was unable to stand and I struggled to get him back into the camper. I knew something drastic had occurred. Early the next morning I drove directly home to Phoenix, and after securing Jato in his fenced yard, I took Luke to the vet. He told me Luke's spine had separated and there was no hope. I hugged Luke and thanked him for our wonderful five years together while the vet's injection ended his pain and his life. Jato's reaction was one of dismay when I returned home without Luke. I had never seen a dog mourn for a loved one the way Jato mourned for Luke.

I experienced reluctance similar to that of the Forest Service Alpine staff to sponsor my public showing of the Mexican wolf slide show in the Coronado National Forest's campgrounds in the Chiricahua area. I inquired of my friend Leon Fisher, Forest Service biologist in the Albuquerque regional office, why the Forest Service was not supporting public educational programs on the Mexican wolf. Fisher agreed that my concerns were legitimate. He said he had had concerns of a similar nature concerning the Region 3 lack of proactive support for all endangered species programs. He told me that he and his staff were preparing a document to be distributed throughout Region 3, informing employees that their cooperation and support for endangered species, including the Mexican wolf, was mandated by Forest Service policies. Unfortunately, Fisher told me later that his document was so thoroughly watered down by his superiors in the Region 3 Albuquerque office that it was rendered absolutely useless. As a result he recommended that I take up the matter with Jay Gore, who worked in Chief Forester Dale Robertson's office in Washington, D.C.

In November 1991, the USFWS had accepted the Phoenix Zoo as a captive-breeding facility for the Mexican wolf. Mike Seidman, senior keeper at the zoo and chief caretaker for the newly arrived Mexican wolves, believed their existing compound was not conducive to breeding. A plan existed for the zoo to build a larger, more heavily vegetated complex to provide a better environment for the mating of wolves. While the current compound was adequate for exhibiting mammals, it provided no privacy. Children frequently leaned over the railing to wave their arms and yell at the wolves.

Phoenix P.A.WS. members were overjoyed at having Mexican wolves in the Phoenix Zoo and agreed that helping the zoo build a new wolf complex would be a great project for us to tackle. Many people put in hours of work on this project, spearheaded by zoo staff Warren Iliff, recently appointed executive director; his manager of development, John Vack; John's program manager, Becky Adams; and from P.A.WS., John Engle, Patty Williams, and me. The Phoenix Zoo and P.A.WS. jointly sponsored community fund-raising projects, in which participants were known as WOLFKEEPERS. About fifty groups in the Phoenix area conducted fund-raising activities and together contributed about $12,000 for the new wolf complex. Ed Eisele, owner of Holsum Bakery and long-time supporter of the zoo, donated $50,000. P.A.WS.'s fund-raiser was a well-attended dinner and auction of wolf memorabilia held at the Scottsdale Plaza Hotel. Organized by members Barbara Boltz and Pam Cook Butler, this event raised $18,000. Warren Parker, former red wolf recovery coordinator from North Carolina, was our keynote speaker, and the late Herb Drinkwater, former mayor of Scottsdale, hosted the event.

The year-long effort culminated in a large rally at the Phoenix Zoo on November 7, 1992, at which we raised $80,000 towards the construction of the Mexican wolf complex, but this amount proved far less than the $300,000 needed to complete the complex. The ground-breaking ceremony was put off until June 12, 1993, and actual construction did not begin until a year later, when Jeff Williamson assumed directorship of the zoo. Williamson focused on the ecological need for increasing the Mexican wolf population and worked tirelessly together with zoo staff and volunteers to build the new breeding complex. He encouraged his development staff to expend the necessary effort to solicit additional donations from large corporations and individuals.

In January 1995, the Phoenix Zoo's two Mexican wolves, Rosa and Chico, were moved to the completed wolf facility and a public grand opening celebration was held. Many dignitaries were on hand to praise the large new area in which more than one hundred native plant species grew in rocky surroundings that resembled the Blue Range Area. A large degree of the credit for the incentive behind the new facility was credited to P.A.WS.'s efforts.

Howling for Wolves

How can one love Creator and not the creation? Nature is called good by the One who makes it—all of it, even the parts we don't understand or find pretty or make use of, the parts that get in our way and sometimes frighten us with their teeth.
—Diane Sylvain, *High Country News*, April 17, 1997

Terry Johnson believed that wolf-howling surveys along the Mexican border should be conducted in answer to many reported sightings. In early December 1992, together with staff from AGFD, in conjunction with USFWS and USFS, Johnson conducted two two-day wolf-howling workshops and surveys in Sierra Vista, Arizona. Sierra Vista lies at about four thousand feet elevation at the foot of the Huachuca Mountains, with the highest point, Miller Peak, at 9,460 feet. Vegetation ranges from pinyon, oak, and juniper up into ponderosa pine and Douglas fir at higher elevations. The lower elevations boast fine grazing lands with native grasses, blue grama, side oats, plains love grass, and blue stems.

Johnson hired Dr. Paul Joslin, conservation and research director for Wolf Haven International, to teach the workshops. Attendees included staff from USFWS, AGFD, USFS, and Animal Damage Control (ADC), and Johnson invited me to attend. During a day-long workshop that preceded the survey, Joslin told us about his success with howling surveys in Canada and in Washington state. He showed us how to use compasses to determine the location of any response. We were to record all responses from wolves, coyotes, owls, cows, or even humans.

We learned how to use parabolic receivers to capture any answers we received. The parabolic receiver was attached to a small cassette player for recording responses. AGFD staff explained the data forms we were to complete for their data bank, which would provide valuable information for their wildlife records. We all made fools of ourselves when Joslin had us line up and howl like wolves.

The local Forest Service staff laid out several survey routes for howling along old wolf runs on the west side of the mountains, frequented by Mexican wolves migrating up from Mexico in earlier years. After dark, each participant and a selected partner were assigned a route for the survey. Laura Dupee, range conservationist from the Sierra Vista Forest Service Ranger Station, agreed to be my partner. After years of working with local ranchers, she knew every one of the routes like a wolf knows its game trails. A few weeks before, Dupee told me she'd seen some Mexican wolves, two adults and a pup, in Red Rock Canyon in the Patagonia Mountains but at the time had no camera for evidence. Tracks obtained later indicated a very large canid, and Larry Allen said that they could have been migratory wolves.

Dupee and I then followed our fifteen-mile route and took turns howling at intervals. We received several coyote howls before the wind came up and made our howls less audible. The Forest Service had equipped each team with a two-way radio so communication could be maintained. At one stop, I howled while Dupee used the receiver and cassette to catch any answer. The answering howls sounded strangely human.

"I think that's some of our howlers," Dupee said. "I'll get on my radio and try to find out who it is. I helped Larry Allen plan these routes, and none of the others should be that close to us."

Dupee contacted the howlers on the radio, who were two ADC men from New Mexico, unfamiliar with the area and completely lost. After she'd provided them with instructions on how to get back to the main road, we completed our route.

The following day we all reported our survey results and played back any questionable howls. One group had a wolf-sounding howl, but a later check on the howl's origin indicated that it had probably been someone's pet wolf-dog. Joslin gave us detailed information about the paw prints of various predators and how best to track them. He also showed samples and pictures of different wildlife species' scat and its contents. As he told us, "Scat happens."

At the end of the workshop, I took Terry Johnson to one side to tell him about an idea I had. "This is something P.A.WS. can get involved with," I said. "Game and Fish needs more data on reported wolf sightings. P.A.WS. can raise funds to provide more equipment and teaching materials for conducting additional workshops and surveys. We can train volunteers who are willing to devote time to learn the process, and then go out on more surveys."

"Sounds good to me," agreed Johnson.

"I think that during the next year, between all of the fairs and festivals we're participating in, we should be able to raise $5,000 for this project," I said.

"That would be great," he concluded.

Despite our many letters and phone call drives, P.A.WS. had not been successful in convincing the powers-that-be in Congress that the Mexican wolf recovery program desperately needed increased funds. After Defenders of Wildlife became involved in the Mexican wolf effort in 1991, when Hank Fischer announced the Mexican wolf compensation plan, Defenders assigned Evan Hirsche, a member of their Washington, D.C., staff, to the Mexican wolf project.

During several long-distance phone calls, Hirsche and I discussed what we needed to do to make Mexican wolf reintroduction a reality. Fischer had told him that taking Congress members or their legislative aides on a tour through wolf country was an effective way to win their support for the needed appropriation. Hirsche asked me about the possibility of scheduling a tour similar to the one I'd told him I'd had with Allen. I thought Allen would cooperate with such a tour and might even arrange for Forest Service vans to convey the participants.

The tour group was to include a few key congressional legislative aides; Michael Spear and other USFWS staff; Allen; Johnson; Susan Larson, president of the Mexican Wolf Coalition of New Mexico; Hirsche; and me.

After I provided Hirsche with all of the principal participants' names, he made most of the contacts. Spear wanted to show the Washington people not only wolf country but also other wildlife projects for which the USFWS wanted federal support. Hirsche arranged a two-day tour that would begin at the Ramada Inn in south Tucson.

Dupee arranged for two vans to carry the group, which grew to include David Parsons, Mexican wolf recovery coordinator; Sam Spiller, Phoenix USFWS office supervisor; and Defenders president Rodger Schlickeisen. Although Hirsche had originally reached agreements with three legislative aides to join the group, only one actually made the trip—Michael Bagley from Washington's Congressman Norm Dicks's (D) office. Hirsche and I were disappointed that the others weren't able to join us.

Friday's drive included a tour of the Santa Cruz riparian-habitat private-lands partnership initiative for neotropical migratory bird conservation, with a tailgate lunch in the riparian habitat. We then drove over to the Buenos Aires National Wildlife Refuge for a program briefing on the masked bobwhite recovery program. Then we toured the Arivaca Creek riparian acquisition and discussed water rights, instream flow, and the wildlife education opportunities available at this site. When we returned to the Buenos Aires refuge, we were greeted with the tantalizing aroma of an outdoor steak fry. Following dinner, we watched storm clouds gather over the Baboquivari Mountains, and then returned to overnight at the Ramada in Tucson.

On Saturday morning we were given a program briefing on the Mexican wolf recovery program by Peter Siminski at ASDM. Siminski conducted our group through the grounds to view all the wildlife and took us to the off-exhibit holding facility, where we were treated to intimate views of their breeding pairs of Mexican wolves.

After lunch in Tucson, we were taken on a tour through historic Mexican wolf habitat in potential reintroduction areas within the Chiricahua Mountains and the Patagonia/Atascosa Mountains. We dined at a cafe in Patagonia and spent the night there at the Stage Stop Inn. The next morning, following a scenic tour of the rugged Huachuca Mountains and grassy rangelands of the San Rafael Valley, we were driven back to Tucson's Ramada Inn, where we went our separate ways.

During this trip I was shocked and sorry to learn that Spear was being transferred from his Region 2 directorship in Albuquerque to become USFWS director of ecological services in Washington, D.C.

"I hate to see you leave now that we finally have things moving for the Mexican wolf," I told Spear.

"It wasn't my choice to leave, " he said. "I wanted to finish my years with the Service and retire in Albuquerque. Just remember that the Mexican wolf will always have a friend in D.C. as long as I'm there."

The tour made Bagley a strong Mexican wolf advocate, and reportedly his glowing descriptions of our tour made other aides sorry they had not participated. Bagley's boss, Congressman Norm Dicks, has remained 100 percent behind our efforts.

Hirsche decided that the only way we were going to convince congressional members of the critical need for them to fund the Mexican wolf project was to visit them in their offices on Capitol Hill. Defenders agreed to sponsor such a trip. Hirsche arranged for representatives from wolf coalitions in Arizona, New Mexico, and Texas to fly to Washington and talk to members of Congress and some agency officials, who could help in obtaining the funds USFWS needed to implement the recovery program.

That February 1993 lobbying trip included Carol Martindale and Bud Lensing from New Mexico, Marcia Sullivan from Texas, and me. We had previously arranged for appointments with our individual state Senators and Representatives and other dignitaries. I recalled what Spear had told me on the congressional tour in 1992, and I made an appointment to talk to him. I also planned to seek out Jay Gore in Forest Service Chief Robertson's office to discuss the problem I had had with regional Forest Service officials disallowing P.A.WS.'s slide show programs.

For the past few years, the federal appropriation for the Mexican wolf project had been stalled at $150,000, and this did not begin to meet the growing needs Parsons had to produce the EIS and hold public hearings. He had no permanent staff in Albuquerque and needed a wildlife biologist to relieve him of the growing mountains of work. Parsons provided me with a verbal wish list and hoped for an appropriation of $500,000.

We made the rounds on Capitol Hill to see our states' Congress members and other key members on both the Senate and House Interior Appropriations Subcommittees. Senator Dennis DeConcini and his staff warmly welcomed our visit. During his term of office prior to his retirement in 1994, he was a staunch supporter of the Mexican wolf reintroduction program. Sometimes we split up, which gave me a chance to see Spear. I reminded him of his promise about being a friend of the Mexican wolf and expressed the urgency for a major increase in the Interior appropriation for the Mexican wolf.

"I think we can free up $400,000 in the appropriation that the Service receives from Interior," he said confidently. Spear

Bud Lensing, Bobbie Holaday, Marcia Sullivan, and Carol Martindale lobbied in Washington, D.C., in 1993. Photo by Maria Cecil, Defenders of Wildlife.

had strong connections with congressional members of the Interior Appropriations Subcommittee and believed that he could set in motion the process to obtain the funding needed to implement Mexican wolf recovery.

While this was not the entire $500,000 Parsons had hoped for, it was a major improvement over $150,000.

At that time the Democrats held a majority in the House, and the chair of the House Interior Appropriations Subcommittee was Illinois Representative Sidney Yates (D). We had a group meeting with Neal Sigmon, Majority staff director for this subcommittee. Hirsche had warned us that while Sigmon was supportive of wolf programs in general, he would be noncommittal and businesslike. I was happy to see wolves staring at us from two pictures hung on the walls of the subcommittee hearing room. When we began the meeting, Sigmon was indeed solemn and stone faced, but I believe our enthusiasm for saving this critically endangered subspecies was contagious because before long, he was smiling. He made no commitment, but as Hirsche expressed later, "I think the meeting went well because Neal seemed unusually positive."

Hirsche's ability to conduct us around Capitol Hill impressed me. He lead us down through the maze of underground walkways in the bowels of these historic buildings, in which our nation's government has been making decisions for years. Walking down the same halls where the Roosevelts, Eisenhower, Kennedy, and others had walked gave me a patriotic thrill I had not expected. Hirsche knew all the congressional aides on a first-name basis, showing that he'd spent a lot of time visiting these offices before. While I had previously lobbied Arizona congress members in their home offices, this was my first time in D.C., and it helped to have someone as competent as Hirsche to guide us.

The $400,000 appropriation later became a reality when the Interior budget for fiscal year '94 was approved. Our lobbying trip had proven successful.

While in Washington, I made an appointment to see Jay Gore. I related to Gore the opposition I had encountered with both the Coronado and Apache National Forest officials when I offered public education programs featuring the USFWS-produced slide show "A Call for the Wild." I said that the USFS should be cooperating, not opposing, offers to provide badly needed public education on the wolf. Jay Gore agreed and recommended that I take the matter up with the chief himself. Unfortunately, Chief Robertson was not in his office at the time, so I planned to correspond with him on the matter.

In my April 10, 1993, letter to the chief, I told him that USFWS was implementing the Mexican Wolf Recovery Plan with the intent of reintroducing the endangered Mexican wolf into appropriate historical locations in Arizona and New Mexico. Our grassroots support group, P.A.WS., wanted to provide educational programs for the public with accurate and timely information about the Mexican wolf.

I went on to describe the refusal of officials in both the Coronado and the Apache National Forests to sponsor public programs where such wolf education would be featured. I mentioned that Leon Fisher, regional program manager for threatened and endangered species, had tried to produce a document to direct all of the Forest Service offices in the region to support the Mexican wolf recovery program, only to have his regional forester water it down and render it useless.

Then I quoted from Section 7 of the ESA:

FEDERAL AGENCY ACTIONS AND CONSULTATIONS.—
(i) The Secretary shall review other programs administered by him and utilize such programs in furtherance of the purposes of this Act. All other Federal agencies shall, in consultation with and with the assistance of the Secretary, utilize their authorities in furtherance of the purposes of this Act by carrying out programs for the conservation of endangered species and threatened species listed pursuant to section 4 of this Act. (p. 16)

In addition, I quoted from the United States Department of Agricultural Forest Service Title 2600—Wildlife, Fish, and Sensitive Plant Habitat Management, where in several places it mandates support for threatened and endangered species:

2670.31—Threatened and Endangered Species
Place top priority on conservation and recovery of endangered, threatened, and proposed species and their habitats through relevant National Forest System, State and Private Forestry, and research activities and programs. (pp. 2670–2)
2670.43—Director of Wildlife and Fisheries
Coordinates Forest Service programs for the conservation of threatened, endangered, proposed, and sensitive

species with other agencies, organizations, and groups concerned with management of and research on those species. (pp. 2670–4)

I also quoted three sections that pertained to regional foresters, forest supervisors, and district rangers, which indicated that the USFS was mandated to support such activities as P.A.WS. was offering with our educational programs.

On May 6, Chief Dale Robertson responded to my letter, expressing appreciation for P.A.WS.'s active support of Mexican wolf recovery. The following excerpts from his letter confirmed the Forest Service's mandates to participate in recovery efforts, increase public awareness, and assist in finding suitable reintroduction sites.

> The Forest Service has a clear responsibility to actively join with the Fish and Wildlife Service (FWS) and State Fish and Game Departments in seeking to recover threatened and endangered species, including the Mexican wolf. . . .
>
> Our involvement in the recovery of the Mexican wolf is based on national policy as directed in the Endangered Species Act of 1973, as amended. The Secretary of Agriculture's policy Department Regulation 9500–4 also clearly directs the FS to conduct activities and programs to assist in the identification and recovery of threatened and endangered plant and animal species. Forest Service policy as stated in the FS Manual is also clear on our responsibility to listed species.

The letter explained the opposition I had encountered when I had offered to provide programs on the Mexican wolf with the following: "Because this is such a controversial and sensitive subject, perhaps some employees have been reluctant to talk about Mexican wolf reintroduction or to appear as taking a proactive approach."

A copy of Chief Robertson's letter was sent to the regional forester in Region 3 and to the various forest supervisors and districts, and I never again encountered resistance to my programs. During later summers, I was invited by staff of Alpine District Forest Service's Public Affairs Officer Bob Dyson to conduct several educational campfire programs that featured "A Call for the Wild."

In May 1993, the Mexican wolf lawsuit filed in 1990 by the Wolf Action Group et al. against the Secretary of the Interior and the Secretary of Defense was finally settled. The defendants had filed a motion to either dismiss because the plaintiffs' claims were moot or to settle with a Summary Judgment. Both the USFWS and the U.S. Army had reversed their previous decisions against Mexican wolf recovery. The USFWS began implementing the Mexican Wolf Recovery Plan, and the U.S. Army agreed to the White Sands Missile Base lands being considered as a reintroduction site as long as alternative sites were considered.

As a part of the New Mexico District Court's May 1993 settlement, a *Stipulated Settlement Agreement* was drawn up that contained several important stipulations. The lawsuit was dismissed without prejudice, and the stipulations included the following:

> Reintroduction of the Mexican wolf as expeditiously as possible. (p. 1)
>
> No later than June 10, 1993 the Service agrees to prepare a time table and estimate of costs for accomplishment of the experimental reintroduction phase. (p. 2)
>
> The Service shall prepare its EIS and render a final decision on the initial experimental release as soon as possible with May 1994 as the target date for a final decision. (p. 2)
>
> Plaintiffs shall establish a committee consisting of representatives of their choice but excluding the Service, to monitor the implementation of the Mexican Wolf Recovery Plan. The Service agrees to consider comments provided by this committee. (p. 4)

A representative from the plaintiffs asked me to serve on this committee, which I did until the wolves were released in 1998.

On July 1, 1993, the USFWS issued the mandated time table, which promised dates of May 1994 for both the draft EIS and the Proposed Rule for Nonessential Experimental Population, and March of 1995 for the final EIS and Final Rule. July 1996 was set as the date for the release of Mexican wolves. These dates became significant in 1996 when the USFWS refused to honor the *Stipulated Settlement Agreement.*

6

Blue Task Force and More Human Howls

Wolves aren't the cause of the changes occurring in the West any more than the rooster's crow is the cause of the sun's rising, but they have become the means by which ranchers can voice their concern about what's happening around them.
—Renee Askins, House Committee on Resources hearing, January 1995

The Notice of Intent to Prepare an Environmental Impact Statement was published in the Federal Register on April 20, 1992. During 1992, the USFWS conducted three meetings to obtain input for the EIS. Any hope of a draft EIS by January 1993, as David Parsons had stipulated in his 1991 time table, appeared slim.

During the October 1992 meeting of the AGF Commission, unanimous approval was granted for the Department to write a Plan for the Reintroduction of the Mexican Wolf in the Blue Range Area. I knew from comments given by people from the Blue Range Area and some members of the Commission that had this been anything but a plan, the vote would have been negative.

I decided to put together a task force in the Blue Range Area, consisting of the various interests and agencies. The federal public hearings and meetings had not permitted free dialogue in a relaxed atmosphere. Even the state meetings, while somewhat freer in format, were officially recorded and, to some attendees, intimidating. Perhaps if we could get local environmentalists to talk directly to local ranchers with agency staff present, such

encounters might produce a better understanding between conflicting parties.

Don Hoffman, of the Alpine District Forest Service, who
would be an energetic environmental member of the task force,
helped me to identify other potential members. It took me
about three months to contact about fifty potential members,
forty of whom agreed to come to at least one meeting. Local
environmentalists were happy for this opportunity to express
their beliefs openly but somewhat timid about doing so in an
area where grazing and timber interests predominated. Ranchers were skeptical but curious about my new approach, which
offered open dialogue. I contacted representatives from the
ranching and timber industries, sportsmen, community leaders, business people, as well as the USFWS, the AGFD, and the
USFS. I never could persuade anyone from the White Mountain
Apache Tribe or San Carlos Apache Tribe to participate.

To all who agreed to come to the first meeting, I sent personal letters, telling them, "I would like to see members enter
this process seeking first to understand the other viewpoints,
and then to have their viewpoint understood. If you believe
that you are so biased against such a dialogue and could only
attend to preach a single agenda, I will understand and appreciate your selecting yourself out of this process."

I went on to ask the candidates, "Can we find enough common threads to be able to explore this subject and conduct
dialogue? Can we address our common concerns of social, eco-
nomical, cultural, and ecological impacts without getting caught
up in emotional issues? Can we overcome our animosities?"

I challenged them with "Can we humans co-exist with the
wolf? Can we cut through all of our emotions and rubbish?
Don't we owe it to ourselves to at least listen to each other's
side and attempt dialogue?"

"You'll have an uncontrollable circus," warned Norris Dodd,
then supervisor of the Pinetop Region 1 office for AGFD.

However, Dodd sent Bob Vahle and Jim Hinkle, both assigned to wildlife management; and Dean Berkey, Forest Service district ranger from Alpine, sent Bob Dyson, recreation and public affairs officer.

Our first meeting was held in April 1993, in Springerville, Arizona. Roxanne Knight, a rancher who owned Reed's Motor Lodge and headed Springerville's board of tourism, agreed to make arrangements and act as host. We met at the community center for a late afternoon and evening meeting. I had made arrangements for another task force member, Jack Husted, owner of Springerville's Round Table Pizza, to bring eight large pizzas, and I had beverages available so we didn't have to break for dinner. The thirty-six attendees included representatives from AGFD, USFWS, USFS, environmental and recreation groups, as well as community and business leaders, sportsmen, timber company representatives, and several ranchers.

The entire meeting was devoted to open dialogue, with Tommie Martin facilitating the discussion. Martin had a ranching background herself, being the daughter of Raymond and Pat Cline of Star Valley, former operators of the 7A Ranch. She had received professional training in meeting facilitation and embraced the principles of team-building dialogue. She remained neutral at the meeting. Nothing was tape-recorded. All participants were allowed to talk as long as they wanted to about what they believed the future landscape of the Blue Range Area should be. Without exception, the environmentalists favored the return of the Mexican wolf, and the ranchers strongly opposed it. Most agency representatives and some local business people remained neutral in their discussion. Dr. Roy Jones, sportsman from Lake Havasu City, made the long drive across the state to say that many hunters would welcome the return of the wolf despite the competition for game animals.

Jim Holder, long-time rancher from Eagle Creek in the lower Blue, said, "I sure wouldn't want wolves back." His wife

Clarice agreed, "We wouldn't be able to let our grandkids play outdoors anymore."

Task force ranchers, Billy and Barbara Marks, who ran 224 cattle on fifty-nine thousand acres of national forest lands, strongly opposed wolves, as did Jim Grammar from the T-Links Ranch. Agency representatives were cautious in their comments not to approve openly or condemn plans for reintroduction, and this was understandable considering they live in an area where wolves are hated.

The five-hour dialogue resulted in a consensus that everyone wanted to hold another meeting. The Marks volunteered to host the July meeting at the Blue schoolhouse, near their home deep in the heart of the Blue Range Area.

As I drove the precipitous switchbacks of the gravel road descending into the lower Blue that July, I gasped at the gargoyle formations of the red rock canyon bordering the Blue River. When I entered the untouched deciduous forest of oak, alder, and sycamore trees that line the river, I felt like I had gone back one hundred years. Few homes are visible from the only road that connects the Blue's residents with the outside world.

We enjoyed a lively morning team-building session that spotlighted both the pros and the cons of the wolves' possible return and various perceptions of wolves' behavior. The group enjoyed a potluck lunch put on by members of the local Cowbelles. In the afternoon, Terry Johnson provided positive reasons for returning the wolf, and Warren Parker, former red wolf recovery coordinator from North Carolina, echoed his support. Parker was visiting Johnson, who invited Parker to attend the meeting.

The Marks had invited a dozen or more of their rancher friends to join in the afternoon session, and one by one they displayed a series of blood-drenched pictures of calves and steer killed by lions. The ranchers told their horror stories about cattle slain by lions.

In October 1993, the task force met in the southern end of the Blue Range Area, in the Clifton County Courthouse. Frank Hayes, district ranger for the USFS, hosted the meeting. Our morning session brought out what each participant wanted to see happen in the Blue. Those favoring the wolf's return pointed out that the Blue Range Area is public land, and the ecosystem is diminished by the lack of wolves to balance wildlife populations. Those opposed expressed fears for their personal safety and their future livelihoods if wolves were reintroduced. Despite lack of agreement, progress was being made in establishing trust among the members who might never see eye-to-eye about wolves.

The afternoon session focused on the remote and rugged Sand Rock allotment, located in the middle of the potential Mexican wolf reintroduction area. For ten years this allotment had been under a nonuse agreement with the Forest Service to allow the deteriorating watershed, range, and wildlife habitat time for recovery. Pat Hanrahan, former range conservationist, who had been instrumental in implementing the ten-year nonuse agreement, stated that only a small portion was ever usable for cattle, and that was located mostly in steep canyon bottoms bordering the stream. He believed cattle never should be returned to the Sand Rock. Nancy Walls, Hayes's range conservationist, reviewed the process for planning future uses of the allotment and provided the status of the re-analysis effort. Data collection was being accomplished using students from Round River Conservation Studies. The ten-year nonuse had already allowed remarkable recovery of willow and cottonwood growth along the banks of the stream. Later recommendations from the Round River studies opposed returning cattle to these recovering riparian areas.

Ruken Jelks III, a holistic rancher from Elgin, Arizona, had flown his private plane to Clifton to urge the Blue Range Area ranchers to welcome the return of wolves, because wolves provoked livestock herding that was beneficial to breaking up the soil for forage growth.

Subsequent meetings featured Hank Fischer of Defenders, describing the effectiveness of their wolf compensation fund; a howling workshop and survey conducted by AGFD staff; and discussions on the forthcoming EIS led by David Parsons of the USFWS. Our discussions exposed growing differences in the opinions on wolves held by the Marks and the Holders, who were considering the possibility of coexisting with predators. Meetings continued all through 1994 and up through June 1995, when the draft version of the EIS was ready for review. No final conclusions or resolutions were ever reached. At least a dozen of the task force members faithfully attended nearly all the meetings.

Jim and Clarice Holder were joined on the task force by their son, Will, and his wife, Jan, who had previously lived in Phoenix and worked for America West Airlines. Will and Jan Holder gave up city life to move to the ranch and run it full time. The old ranch quarters were badly run down, and the young Holders made an abrupt adjustment from their cushy surroundings in Phoenix to having to refurbish the ranch house and the nearby bunkhouse. To make matters more difficult, at the time of the move, they were expecting their first child.

For years, hired hands had operated the ranch for Will's parents, who lived in Safford, where Jim was an eye doctor. Much of the land had been neglected and in some areas abused. Will and Jan Holder decided that the ranch's future management plan could not continue traditional grazing practices.

They told task force members that their eyes had been opened to the fact that holism meant managing for the whole, and that would have to include existing with wolves, if they returned. Other ranchers expressed strong opposition to this theory, pointing out their long siege of losing livestock to lions. The Holders countered that they had decided against killing any predators, including lions, but other ranchers scoffed at the idea, adding that it would never work. It was clear that no love was lost between these ranching families.

During the final meeting in June 1995, a few ranchers were angry and said I had betrayed them. They must have hoped that they had demonstrated that wolf reintroduction was a mistake. They said the task force had failed in providing anything for the Blue area ranchers. Some of these ranchers had recently been informed by the USFS that their cattle numbers were going to be severely cut, and perhaps they needed an outlet for their anger. I felt rewarded for having created the task force when other ranchers agreed that whatever the future held in regard to wolf reintroduction, our open dialogue had helped in providing a better understanding between conflicting factions.

The real success story was gaining full support from the Holders. As our task force dialogue continued over more than two years, the entire Holder family abandoned the usual rancher hatred of wolves and said that they would tolerate their presence. By the time we disbanded the task force in 1995, Will and Jan Holder, as well as Will's parents, were supporting the wolf's return: "Our management plan allows us to coexist with predators, and that includes wolves," said Will Holder at our final meeting.

In October 1995, Will testified in favor of Mexican wolf reintroduction at a USFWS public hearing in Phoenix. He said, "With our management plan, we frequently rotate livestock to avoid predators. Since we stopped killing predators, we've had little depredation, and we plan to coexist with wolves."

During all these activities, P.A.WS. had been holding meetings and participating in many events where we provided educational outreach and sold wolf memorabilia. We accomplished our goal to raise $5,000 during 1993 to pay for more wolf-howling workshops, teaching materials, and equipment needed on the howling surveys. In July of 1993, P.A.WS. paid for Paul

Joslin of Wolf Haven International to teach another howling workshop, which we held at the Buenos Aires National Wildlife Refuge. Thea Ulen, outdoor recreation planner for the refuge, hosted the event attended by twenty-five howlers. Buenos Aires staff laid out a dozen or more survey routes.

Ulen's husband, who worked for the U.S. Border Patrol, notified other patrol officers to be on the lookout for the howlers' vehicles on back roads. These roads are also frequented by drug smugglers from Mexico. I brought all the food and was chief cook and bottle washer for the group. Participants chose partners, and I chose Thea, who planned to keep in touch with the howlers via her truck radio.

It was a clear, quiet night with a nearly full moon. At one point Ulen parked on a high plateau outside of Arivaca, where she could attempt radio contact with the other howlers. Bright stars poked holes through heavens' ceiling to provide light for us. I thought I'd try a howl from this high point. I received a rapturous response from a chorus of coyotes. I had communicated with God's dogs!

The next day we shared results, which again indicated no wolves but a lot of coyotes and other night creatures. Many of the new howlers returned to conduct five or six follow-up surveys in the Buenos Aires area.

In 1993, Johnson offered Warren Parker the position of AGFD wolf biologist for the Mexican wolf project. In July, when Parker had accompanied Johnson to the Blue Area Wolf Task Force meeting held at the Blue school, he had had congenial discussions with several of the local ranchers. After the meeting, Johnson had told me, "I'm convinced Warren will accept the position." However, after stalling Johnson for nearly a year, Parker declined.

Johnson immediately resumed the search for a wolf biologist. After interviewing and rejecting many candidates in his search for the right one, he settled on Dan Groebner. Groebner had performed wolf-tracking surveys in Wisconsin with the Earth Watch organization for a few years, and presented wolf programs for the International Wolf Center in Ely, Minnesota. Groebner had earned his bachelor's degree in wildlife management from the University of Wisconsin at Stevens Point and his master's in wildlife management from Northern Michigan University at Marquette, Michigan.

Groebner and his wife, Ann, moved to Arizona in January 1994, with his wife expecting a baby within a few months. They somehow had the impression that they would soon move to the White Mountain area following preliminary work in Phoenix. Terry Johnson had no idea why they held this belief, as such a move would have been ill advised. No official go-ahead had been given by either the USFWS or the AGFD for the reintroduction of the Mexican wolf into the Blue.

For several years I had written letters to Defenders president Rodger Schlickeisen, concerning the need for a representative in the Southwest. I had strongly recommended Craig Miller for this position. In December 1993, Defenders hired him as their Southwest representative. Miller and I celebrated by dining out with Bob Ferris, conservation species director, who worked out of Defenders's Washington office and would be Miller's boss. Soon after Miller landed his position with Defenders, he discontinued nearly all communications with me.

Early in 1994, P.A.WS. presented AGFD with the final $3,000 to fund howling workshops, teaching materials, and howling equipment for surveys. Dan Groebner conducted wolf-howling workshops and surveys in Patagonia and Douglas, Arizona, during 1994, and at Hannagan Meadow, near Alpine, Arizona, in 1995, using the funding provided by P.A.WS.

P.A.WS. member Tammy Anderson, a registered nurse, offered

her assistance in contacting trained howlers for wolf-howling surveys wherever and whenever the AGFD believed they were needed. This took a large load off my shoulders, as coordinating such surveys took hours of calling and making arrangements. Anderson had difficulty in limiting survey participation to only trained howlers.

I began to receive reports from some participants that the surveys were not emphasizing data gathering as much as the camaraderie around the campfire that followed. Data forms were incomplete or inaccurate, making them worthless for AGFD's data files. I discussed the situation with Johnson, and he decided that we should curtail any further surveys. "We'll schedule one more workshop conducted by Dan at which all untrained howlers can obtain the necessary training. After that, any survey participation will be limited to trained howlers only."

Mounting tension with his superiors at the AGFD offices, in addition to Groebner's and his wife's dislike of living in Phoenix, became irresolvable. In fall 1995, he accepted a permanent position in the Pinetop Region 1 office of AGFD. In the new position, as endangered species specialist, he was no longer the Mexican wolf biologist. Johnson had to find a new candidate for that position.

I made arrangements for a final wolf-howling workshop and survey in June 1996, to be taught by Groebner, prior to the end of his official duties as wolf biologist. The workshop was held at AGFD's Sipe White Mountain Wildlife area near Springerville, Arizona, with a survey conducted in the Blue Range Area. I persuaded Anderson to facilitate the workshop, giving her an opportunity to enhance her leadership abilities. Over twenty-five participants howled for hours in the wilds of White Mountain forests, but only coyotes and cows responded.

Chico, the Phoenix Zoo's alpha male wolf. Photo by
Robin Silver.

Storm clouds over Baboquivari Peak near Buenos Aires National Wildlife Refuge. Photo by Mike Seidman.

Mexican wolf recovery program needed funds to free captive wolves. Photo courtesy of the U.S. Fish and Wildlife Service.

Gnarled red rock formations border the Blue River. Photo by Don Hoffman.

Rancher Will Holder spoke in support of the Mexican wolves. Photo by Chris Rossic.

A captive Mexican wolf waiting for freedom. Photo courtesy of the
U.S. Fish and Wildlife Service.

P.A.W.S. participated at Tempe Art Festival to raise funds for Mexican wolves. Photo by Chris Rossie.

Sevilleta National Wildlife Refuge Mexican wolf–holding pens. Photo by George Andrejko, Arizona Game and Fish Department.

Lower Blue Range area near Eagle Creek. Photo by Chris Rossie.

The Phoenix Zoo's alpha female, Rosa, with her pup. Photo by Pamela Newton.

Two of Rosa's pups were later released in the Blue. Photo by Pamela Newton.

Bobbie Holaday speaking at teachers' workshop. Photo by
Chris Rossie.

Captive Mexican wolves exhibiting pack reunion behavior. Photo by George Andrejko, Arizona Game and Fish Department.

One of three wolves awaiting the trip to freedom. Photo by George Andrejko, Arizona Game and Fish Department.

Terry Johnson (left) and David Parsons ready Sevilleta wolves for transfer to the Blue. Photo by George Andrejko, Arizona Game and Fish Department.

Upper Blue Range area under a blanket of snow. Photo by George Andrejko, Arizona Game and Fish Department.

Interior Secretary Bruce Babbitt addressed the celebration on the eve of the Campbell Blue release. Photo by David Bluestein.

The Campbell Blue yearling female wolf dashed out of her crate to become the poster wolf with this photo. She would later become the alpha female of the Francisco pack. Photo by George Andrejko, Arizona Game and Fish Department.

Volunteer pen-sitter took a quick picture of a penned wolf after he brought water and food. Photo by Will Stefanov.

Acclimation-pen gates were opened on March 29, 1998. Photo by George Andrejko, Arizona Game and Fish Department.

Informative kiosks were established to educate the visiting public.
Photo by George Andrejko, Arizona Game and Fish Department.

Wolves often dispersed to remote areas and later rejoined their pack.
Photo by George Andrejko, Arizona Game and Fish Department.

Captive Mexican wolf pup similar to the one born to the Campbell Blue pair. Photo courtesy of the U.S. Fish and Wildlife Service.

Mexican wolves struggled to survive during 1998. Photo by George Andrejko, Arizona Game and Fish Department.

Diane Boyd-Heger (center rear) and Duane Shroufe (left rear) observed other unidentified Mexican wolf project staff open crate of New Campbell Blue female. Photo by George Andrejko, Arizona Game and Fish Department.

Val Asher used telemetry to monitor the wolves. Photo by David Bluestein.

Project staff loaded Mexican wolves into panniers for mule ride to a remote release area. Photo by George Andrejko, Arizona Game and Fish Department.

Project staff loaded pannier holding a wolf on mule's back. Photo by George Andrejko, Arizona Game and Fish Department.

Wolves were carried from mules to a mesh pen. Photo by George Andrejko, Arizona Game and Fish Department.

Wolves with fluorescent-taped collars easily broke out of mesh pens and ran free. Photo by George Andrejko, Arizona Game and Fish Department.

Early each morning, Will Holder gathers his herd for pasture rotation. Photo courtesy of Phoenix Newspapers, Inc.

Pups like these captive ones are born yearly to released wolves.
Photo courtesy of U.S. Fish and Wildlife Service.

The Environmental Impact Statement Process
Drags On

If the wolf is to survive, the wolf haters must be outnumbered. They must be outshouted, outfinanced, and outvoted. Their narrow and biased attitude must be outweighed by an attitude based on an understanding of natural processes. Finally their hate must be outdone by a love for the whole of nature, for the unspoiled wilderness, and for the wolf as a beautiful, interesting, and integral part of both.
—L. David Mech, *The Wolf*

During April 1994, Defenders of Wildlife again sponsored leaders from Arizona, New Mexico, and Texas to lobby congressional members in support of the Interior appropriation for the ESA. Mary Beth Beetham, Defenders's Capitol Hill lobbyist, directed our congressional schedule. The attitude on Capitol Hill was not as optimistic as it had been the year before, and even Michael Spear, director of ecological services for the USFWS, showed less enthusiasm. He believed that the EIS must be completed before we could expect any increase in funds. His assessment proved correct, and funds for the Mexican wolf program did not increase in the federal fiscal year 1995 budget.

David Parsons was given some help in the Albuquerque office when in July 1994, the USFWS hired Wendy Brown as wildlife biologist. Brown received her bachelor's degree in wildlife management from the University of New Mexico and her master's in wildlife management from Texas A&M. Most of her career had involved fieldwork and research for the USFWS, none of which involved wolves.

At the October 1994 meeting of the AGF Commission, the Department's Proposed Cooperative Reintroduction Plan for the Mexican Wolf in Arizona was approved. The approval called for the plan to be submitted as an alternative in the forthcoming USFWS draft EIS.

That same month, Parsons issued another time schedule for the publication of the draft and final EIS. This schedule called for the draft EIS to be released to the public in February 1995, with the final EIS to be released to the public in November 1995.

In January 1995, we were given a little comic relief when Arizona State House Representative Jeff Groscost (R) of Mesa offered House Bill 2548, calling for a bounty on wolves. His bill amended the Arizona Revised Statutes by adding a section relating to predatory animal control, stating, "The Department may pay a reward of not more than five hundred dollars for each wolf *(Canis lupus)* that is killed in this state." The bill went on to list criteria the person claiming the reward must fulfill.

I was astounded by Groscost's bill because the fine for killing an endangered species could go as high as $100,000 and/or a year in jail. Linda Valdez, an editor for the *Arizona Republic,* cleverly discredited Groscost's ludicrous bill in an editorial titled "Give That Man a Prize."

The editorial proclaimed that Representative Jeff Groscost must be vying for the Sierra Club's environmental award, because he was doing "a heck of a job" publicizing environmental issues. Valdez referred first to his initiating a legislative bill to make legal the raising and selling of Gila monsters.

"Now it's wolves," she continued, adding that Groscost wanted to award a $500 bounty for each wolf hide turned in to the Game and Fish Department. Talk about a stroke of genius!

"What better way to raise the public's consciousness about an endangered species that was extirpated from Arizona in part because of such human-made assaults as bounties. Groscost deserves hearty thanks for bringing the subject so forcefully into the open for debate."

Fortunately, Arizona State Representative Becky Jordan (R), then chair of the House Natural Resources Subcommittee, tabled both ridiculous bills before any action could be taken on them.

In the fall of 1994, Hank Fischer told me that Defenders needed to increase the wolf compensation fund from $100,000 to $200,000 to cover the combined needs of both the Rocky Mountain area and the Southwest wolf projects. Defenders commissioned artist Cheyenne McAffee to design a large, colorful southwestern-style art poster as a fund-raising vehicle, and at my suggestion, Fischer arranged for P.A.WS. to receive copies to sell in support of Defenders's needs.

P.A.WS. made plans to conduct a fund-raising campaign during 1995 to raise $5,000 towards Defenders's goal. In addition to selling posters, P.A.WS. obtained Defenders's permission to produce at our cost a quantity of T-shirts bearing McAffee's colorful design. Member David Bluestein created an attractive order form for the posters and T-shirts, and copies of the form were distributed by P.A.WS. volunteers throughout Arizona. Defenders's posters and our T-shirts sold like hot cakes, and by the end of 1995, we had raised the $5,000.

The 1995 spring lobbying trip sponsored by Defenders of Wildlife encountered stiff resistance to any budget increases for endangered species. This attitude reflected the depressing changes affecting all environmental programs when the right-wing Republican majority took over Congress following the November 1994 election.

The long-awaited USFWS draft EIS finally appeared in late June 1995, two years after Parson's originally scheduled date. It described five alternatives concerning the reintroduction, including one of no action at all. The Service-recommended

Alternative A called for Mexican wolves to be reintroduced under the nonessential-experimental classification of the ESA. The nonessential-experimental classification had been amended to the ESA to provide the administering agency greater flexibility in management of species in recovery programs than was provided under full protection. This classification allowed for moving or even destroying problem animals to expedite the overall success of the reintroduction process. The USFWS recommended releasing fifteen pairs or family groups into the Blue Range Wolf Recovery Area (BRWRA), distributed over seven thousand square miles over a seven-year period until the year 2005. The USFWS recovery objective was a permanent population of one hundred Mexican wolves in the wild, and, if needed to fulfill that population, up to five pairs or family groups might be released into the backup area, the White Sands Missile Range.

Parsons and Brown conducted a series of fourteen open houses in Arizona, New Mexico, and Texas, assisted by other staff from the USFWS and AGFD. These meetings allowed attendees to learn more about the draft EIS and ask questions concerning the alternatives. The open houses were fairly well attended, with those held in rural areas affected by the release reflecting more opposition than in urban areas.

Johnson briefed the AGF Commission on the provisions in the draft EIS at their August 1995 meeting in Pinetop, and it appeared that the majority of the five-person Commission opposed the recommended alternative.

Later the same month, a USFWS press release announced that both the Ghost Ranch and the Aragon lines of captive wolves, whose blood samples had undergone intensive DNA studies, had been declared pure Mexican wolves. This added eighteen wolves to the captive population, bringing the total to 137.

In 1987, Dennis Parker had written a paper entitled "Southwest Wolves: Discussion of Their Taxonomical Arrangement, an Examination of the Ancestry of Captive-Bred Lines and a Current Field Investigation Pertaining to the Status of the Mexican Gray Wolf *(Canis lupus baileyi)* in Southeastern Arizona." The document carried details of his field studies on the Mexican wolf and included maps showing the ranges of the three subspecies, *Canis lupus baileyi, Canis lupus mogollonensis,* and *Canis lupus monstrabilus.* Parker had never found a publisher for his paper, but copies were informally distributed among people interested in wolves. Most wolf scientists recognized Ron Nowak's more recent recategorizing of the original twenty-four North American subspecies down to five, with the previous three wolf subspecies considered as *Canis lupus baileyi.*

In 1995, Parker produced an undated, unpublished, abbreviated version of his original document. He wrote it in response to the draft version of the Mexican wolf EIS and printed it under the auspices of Applied Ecosystem Management, Inc. He titled this new version *Reintroduction of the Mexican Wolf: Instrument of Recovery or Instrument of Demise?* The paper claimed that reintroduction would not conserve the Mexican wolf because no examples existed of gray wolf reintroduction using captive-raised animals. The paper stated that the genetic base of the captive population had resulted in inbreeding depression because it consisted of only two founding males and a founding female, too narrow a base to produce an animal that could survive in the wild. Further he claimed that there were still wild Mexican wolves present in the wilds of the Southwest, and an experimental population released in the area was contrary to the ESA. Parker insisted that the *mogollonensis* subspecies, not the *baileyi,* had occupied the range for which reintroduction was being recommended. He did not accept the more recent subspecies realignment by Nowak, nor the results of DNA studies of UCLA's Dr. Robert Wayne, which had proved the genetic purity of both the Ghost Ranch and the Aragon line of Mexican wolves. The paper claimed that these lines exhibited "presence of pronounced dog tendencies." His conclusions stated that only the "no wolf" alternative offered in the draft EIS was acceptable.

It was hard to understand why Parker would dispute the findings of Ron Nowak and Robert Wayne, two experts who held zoological doctorates. His second paper was widely distributed among organizations and citizens opposing Mexican wolf reintroduction and provoked wide-reaching controversy as to the stability and feasibility of the Mexican wolf recovery program.

Other recognized scientific papers proving the genetic purity of the captive wolves were published on this subject at about the same time and included the following:

- "Genetic Evaluation of the Three Captive Mexican Wolf Lineages and Consequent Recommendations," by Philip Hedrick, Department of Zoology of Arizona State University, funded by AGFD's Heritage funds, and distributed by ASU in July 1995, with the content later appearing in the third article listed here.
- "Relationships and Genetic Purity of the Endangered Mexican Wolf Based on Analysis of Microsatellite Loci," by Jaime Garcia-Moreno, Marjorie D. Matocq, Michael S. Roy, Eli Geffen, and Robert K. Wayne, published in *Conservation Biology* in April 1996.
- "Genetic Evaluation of the Three Captive Mexican Wolf Lineages," by Philip W. Hedrick, Philip S. Miller, Eli Geffen, and Robert Wayne, published in *Zoo Biology* in January 1997.

Unfortunately, these articles, although published in credible journals, did not receive the widespread attention Parker's paper had among those opposed to the return of the wolf. The ensuing reaction to Parker's "no wolf" conclusion among the opposing citizenry mandated dissemination of scientific proof to squelch the paper's misconceptions.

Parsons asked for a peer review of Parker's paper, and fifteen wolf scientists, including Parsons, reviewed and commented on the document. The reviewers included most of the top wolf experts in the country.

The review results revealed agreement that although some of Parker's claims might warrant further study, the overall reaction was a conclusive rebuttal of his theories. A sampling from the review comments (Parsons 1995) follows:

> As to the success of captive-raised wolves:
> Parker chooses to not mention the very successful reintroduction from captive-raised animals of another large North American canid, the red wolf. Although not a gray wolf, the successful red wolf reintroduction presents a reasonable model for a successful gray wolf reintroduction. (Siminski p. 2)
>
> As to the genetic base question:
> Parker does not reference the recent molecular genetic analysis done by myself [Dr. Robert Wayne] and colleagues [accepted for publication in *Conservation Biology*] that specifically addresses the genetic relationships of the three Mexican wolf captive lineages and their suitability for reintroduction. (Wayne p. 3)
>
> The certified captive population now has seven founders. Parker was advised of this development prior to the issuance of his paper. (Parsons p. 3)
>
> As to whether the captive Mexican wolf population viability and suitability for reintroduction met the requirements of the ESA:
> Our recent results show that the genetic variability (heterozygosity) of the captive certified Mexican gray wolves is not significantly less than that in wild populations of gray wolves. (Wayne p. 8)
>
> For inbreeding depression to happen, the increased homozygosity caused by inbreeding needs to result in an increased expression of deleterious recessive traits. This has not happened (in the captive population of Mexican wolves). (Siminski p. 6)
>
> As to questions of purity and inbreeding raised by the addition of the ASDM-GR and Aragon Zoo lines of wolves:

The molecular evidence for microsatellite loci (Hedrick, 1996, Garcia-[Moreno] et al., 1995) show no indication that the male founder of the ASDM-GR line had ancestry from a dog or a wolf-dog hybrid. (Hedrick p. 11)

A general conclusion:

The paper appears to have been written not as an objective analysis but to try to discredit the proposed Mexican wolf reintroduction. I say this because the paper misinterprets or misconstrues the literature it cites, and it ignores other salient studies, all in ways that lead to a conclusion against Mexican wolf reintroduction. (Mech p. 12)

Results of Parson's peer review were published by the USFWS under the title *A Critical Review of an Unpublished, Undated Paper by Dennis Parker (Biologist, Applied Ecosystem Management, Inc.) Titled Reintroduction of the Mexican Wolf: Instrument of Recovery or Instrument of Demise?* The review was made available to the public and totally refuted the misconceptions in Parker's paper.

Meanwhile, construction had begun of a large five-pen holding facility at the Sevilleta National Wildlife Refuge in New Mexico to serve as a preconditioning area for candidate Mexican wolves, before their transfer to the final acclimation pens in the Blue Range Area. Plans were under way to move five pairs of healthy young wolves considered nonessential to the captive population's gene pool in the Sevilleta facility late in December 1996.

Despite the fourteen open houses provided by the USFWS in Arizona, New Mexico, and Texas, ranchers in all three states demanded that formal public hearings be held, claiming that the Service had not provided adequate public notice for the open houses. Parsons scheduled three public hearings for early October 1995; one in Alpine, Texas, where most attendees opposed el lobo's return, one in Albuquerque, New Mexico, and one in Phoenix, Arizona. Both of the latter audiences were overwhelmingly pro-wolf.

Prior to these meetings in October 1995, Rob Smith, Southwest representative for the Sierra Club, was able to free up funds to bring Kent Dana, his Mission Wolf team, and three wolves to Phoenix for a series of public programs in several schools and at the Phoenix library conference hall. School children ooohed and aaahed when the wolves licked their faces and howled. I harbored mixed emotions about the message given by friendly ambassador wolves mixing with the public in such close proximity, because wolves are wild animals and should not be represented as tame animals that might make good pets. However, at this point, any positive media attention we could create for the Mexican wolf program was beneficial. At all of the public appearances, I urged those present, "Be sure to attend the upcoming important public hearings to be held by the U.S. Fish and Wildlife Service and the Arizona Game and Fish Department."

At the USFWS October Phoenix hearing, with help from the Grand Canyon chapter of the Sierra Club, P.A.WS. staged a prehearing rally, coordinated by Renee Guillory, featuring prominent supporters of wolf reintroduction. These included Warren Iliff, Peter Siminski, and Will Holder. At the formal hearing, only a few speakers opposed the reintroduction of the Mexican wolf, but quite a few environmentalists opposed the nonessential-experimental classification set forth in Alternative A, and recommended Alternative C, which called for full protection.

Many of my environmental friends often asked me how I could support the less protective classification stipulated in Alternative A. I responded, "I respect your adherence to the purity of the full protection provided in Alternative C, and if this were a perfect world, I would support it. If we hold out for full protection, Mexican wolf reintroduction will never happen. You may go to heaven with your purity, but I want to see wolves on the ground in my lifetime."

Two days later, the October 1995 AGF Commission was to vote on the proposed draft EIS recommendation. We were afraid the Commission might oppose further support for the USFWS proposed reintroduction of the Mexican wolf. P.A.WS. members attended in large numbers, as did other Arizona wolf supporters. Beth Woodin, who had served on the AGF Commission from 1990 until 1995, had made two officials from the ASDM aware of the significance of the Commission meeting. At the October AGF Commission meeting, these officials, Arch Brown, president of the board of trustees, and David Hancocks, executive director of ASDM, provided strong testimony in support of returning the Mexican wolf. In addition, many environmentalists and P.A.WS. members testified on behalf of the Mexican wolf. There were, of course, the usual voices of opposition from wolf-fearing ranchers and hunters.

The Commission passed, by a vote of three to two, a motion by Commissioner Mike Golightly that stated, "I recommend that the Commission vote to support Alternative A of the U.S. Fish and Wildlife Service's draft Environmental Impact Statement prescribing reintroduction of the Mexican wolf into White Sands National Proving Grounds." He went on to explain that this recommendation was contingent upon a list of provisions regarding satisfaction of the Commission's list of concerns, publication of a Proposed Rule for Nonessential Experimental Population, and provision in the final EIS for an adaptive management program that would determine subsequent reintroductions. (The motion is recorded in the AGF Commission transcript of the October meeting.) Commissioners voting in favor of the proposal, besides Mike Golightly, were Fred Belman, a Tucson attorney, and Art Porter, of Arthur Porter Construction. Opposed were Herb Guenther, from Tacna, and Nonie Johnson, from Snowflake.

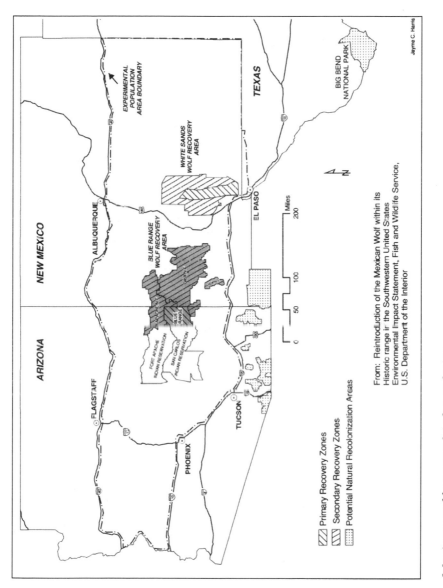

From: Reintroduction of the Mexican Wolf within its
Historic range in the Southwestern United States
Environmental Impact Statement, Fish and Wildlife Service,
U.S. Department of the Interior

Mexican wolf geographic boundaries.

I came away from the meeting elated, but the next day I received phone calls by the score from wolf advocates disappointed with the AGF Commission's proposal because it didn't call for the initial reintroduction to take place in the Blue Range Area. They thought that the Commission and Department were abdicating their responsibility for Mexican wolf reintroduction. Nothing could have been further from the truth, because the vote had been a victory, not a defeat. The Commission had been very close to voting down any further AGFD participation in the Mexican wolf recovery program. This was the first time any game and fish commission voted affirmatively for any wolf reintroduction program. Those who felt dejected failed to remember the wording of the draft EIS Alternative A, which the Commission had supported: "Based on specific decision criteria, the U.S. Fish and Wildlife Service proposed to reintroduce Mexican wolves, classified as nonessential experimental, into the White Sands Wolf Recovery Area or the Blue Range Wolf Recovery Area, followed by a second reintroduction into the other area if necessary and feasible" (Sec. 2, p. 7). A White Sands reintroduction would be limited to only twenty wolves, not a sufficient population to fulfill the USFWS required population of one hundred wolves (pp. 2–7). Obviously, a wolf reintroduction in the Blue Range Area would be mandatory.

Terry Johnson told me my reaction to the meeting's outcome was correct, and said that the commissioners told him it was P.A.WS.'s persistent and reasonable testimony during years of Commission meetings that resulted in the three-to-two vote.

Beth Woodin had long been a friend of the Mexican wolf. As a commissioner she provided strong support, and her enthusiasm and knowledge on the role of wolves in the ecosystem helped convince Golightly to support the program. She said that Belman told her that the testimony of the ASDM dignitaries had influenced his vote.

Prior to serving on the Commission, Woodin had been a

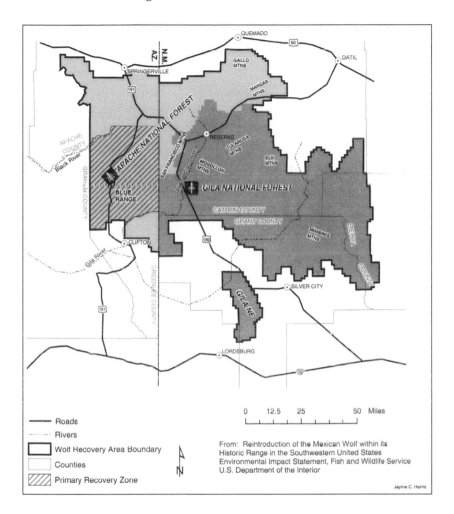

Blue Range Wolf Recovery Area.

trustee for the Arizona chapter of the Nature Conservancy from 1980 until 1992 and, since completing her Commission term, had served on the conservancy's advisory council. She had also served on the ASDM board and long been associated with the museum, as her husband, Bill, had been executive director from 1954 until 1971, when he retired.

New Mexico's Game and Fish Department director, Jerry Maracchini, was unhappy with the AGF Commission's proposal for the initial release of Mexican wolves to take place at White Sands. In a letter to Nancy Kaufman, regional director of the USFWS, he declared that his agency "currently sees no potential Mexican wolf-release site in New Mexico that provides both the biological and societal elements necessary—valid tests of wild wolf behavior and local residents' support." He added that the White Sands area would not be suitable and expressed concern about reduction in deer populations. The New Mexico Game and Fish Commission concurred with Maracchini's decision.

On October 27, 1995, Governor Fife Symington expressed his opposition to wolf reintroduction because wolves would be hazardous to the health and welfare of the people in Arizona. His letter to Parsons said that a leading medical expert in Arizona had told him that a significant human health risk would likely arise if wolves returned to the Southwest. The reintroduced wolves would undoubtedly roam to Mexico and contract rabies, an almost universally fatal disease, and carry it back to the United States. Aggressive rabid wolves would then spread the disease to humans, either through direct attacks or indirect transmission from other animals bitten by the wolves.

Governor Symington's letter went on to explain the negative economic impact that rural Arizonans would suffer from reduced hunting activity and expensive losses of cattle. He cited "strong consensus in the scientific community" that the narrow genetic base of the captive population rendered it unsuitable for reintroduction into the wilds. He suspected that the USFWS would alter the nonessential-experimental status to fully endangered. He feared that the USFWS would not hold to the population target of one hundred wolves, and the population of wolves could rise substantially. Finally he claimed that the proposed reintroduction was in conflict with the provisions of the ESA.

Within a week of receiving the Symington letter, Parsons received an equally opposing letter from Gary Johnson, Governor of New Mexico, claiming that the proposed reintroduction had ignored the National Environmental Policy Act and that he was not willing to leverage his state's financial security against a mixture of folklore and anecdotes.

USFWS staff considered these letters together with the thousands of letters and comments gathered during the draft EIS comment period that became a part of public records. They found both governors' letters lacked credibility and warranted no changes in the EIS.

8

Just Too Muddy to Plow

Strength does not come from physical capacity. It comes from in-
domitable will.
                    —Mahatma Gandhi

The year 1996 opened with a surprising honor at the annual
AGF Commission awards banquet, where I was presented with
the award for 1995 Environmentalist of the Year. It was unprecedented for a state game and fish commission to publicly
honor a lead spokesperson for wolf reintroduction. Art Porter,
outgoing chair, who presented the award, congratulated me on
my many years of hard work for an endangered species, and
added that the Commission appreciated my moderate demeanor
concerning Mexican wolf reintroduction at public hearings and
Commission meetings. In that moment, I ascended to a mountain peak, after years of slogging through the muddy mire of
opposition.

I soon descended from that exhilaration during January
when, in order to continue a healthy relationship with the
ACGA, I attempted to schedule a meeting with their new president. After I made several attempts, it was clear that the association was not interested in scheduling such a meeting. ACGA
representatives remarked at an AGF Commission meeting that
the draft EIS failed to meet the criteria established in the 1991
resolution, but they gave no indication as to which criteria had
not been met. It was disheartening to see that much of the
progress that we had made in 1991 with the ACGA had deteri-
orated following the influx of the anti-environmental influence.

Chapters of the People for the West were blossoming in many rural communities, setting back the cooperative progress previously made by the ACGA. Coalition of Counties groups, dominated by grazing, mining, and logging interests, were forming throughout western New Mexico and eastern Arizona. These groups soon caused a shift to the far right in the Arizona State Legislature. This was particularly painful as we saw defeat of an education bill encouraging teachers to increase environmental emphasis in the classroom. Legislative lobbyists, such as Raena Honan and Sandy Bahr from the Sierra Club, fought valiantly to promote pro-environmental legislation, but all too often they were overwhelmed by the ultraconservative forces that dominated the legislature.

Later in January, I heard a rumor that Interior Secretary Bruce Babbitt would never approve the final EIS before the fall '96 election, and I found such an accusation of Secretary Babbitt appalling. The rumor implied that politicians were making a pawn of the endangered Mexican wolf. I hoped this attitude was not the official stand of others in the USFWS in Washington, D.C.

I had an opportunity to follow up on this alarming rumor during a March lobbying trip to Washington, D.C. Pam Kelly from Texas, Cindy Roper from New Mexico, and I made the usual rounds on Capitol Hill with Craig Miller and Mary Beth Beetham of Defenders. Bob Ferris, conservation species director for Defenders, had scheduled a meeting for all of us with the top Washington USFWS officials. Among those present were John Rogers, acting director; Jamie Clark, appointed ecological services director after Michael Spear left to become the new regional director for the Northwest; Dan Ashe, director of external affairs; and Lesli Gray of USFWS legislative affairs. During our discussion about the delays in the Mexican wolf program, I brought up the rumor that I'd heard about Secretary Babbitt and bluntly asked if this reflected the attitude of the Washington office of Fish and Wildlife. The officials assured me that there was no such intent on the part of anyone in the Washington office to delay the program, and they expressed what seemed to be genuine enthusiasm for having wolves on the ground as soon as possible. They all spoke with such apparent sincerity that I naively believed them.

We concentrated our lobbying on Congress members from both political parties who had a history of supporting endangered species efforts. It became clear that while most support came from Democrats, saving wild critters was often a nonpartisan issue, and we received strong support from a number of moderate Republicans.

Our Washington lobbying helped secure a large increase in the federal Interior appropriation for all ecological services and earmarked a $2 million increase for endangered species programs for fiscal year '97. When the USFWS sliced up the budget pie, the Mexican wolf program received an adequate budget of $500,000. The increased Interior budget also included funds to allow salary increases for David Parsons and his Albuquerque staff.

Parsons had received and reviewed thousands of comments on the draft EIS and made the necessary revisions for the final version. He sent a draft of the final EIS to Nancy Kaufman for her review before getting it published. In early April, Parsons announced that the June publication date for the final EIS again would be delayed. He offered no explanation other than the fact that internal reviews were holding up the process.

Wolf advocates in Arizona and New Mexico were getting restless. Defenders, Audubon, Sierra Club, P.A.WS., the Southwest Center for Biodiversity, and other environmental groups consulted with Attorney Grove Burnett, who had handled the previous Mexican wolf lawsuit. We agreed that if the USFWS continued to delay the final EIS, we must take legal action.

On April 19, 1996, Burnett sent Kaufman a letter, which stated:

> The *Stipulated Settlement Agreement* entered into by the parties on May 21, 1993 imposed a number of duties on the U.S. Fish and Wildlife Service ("Service") in connection with the implementation of the Mexican Wolf Recovery Plan. Although the Service has fulfilled many of its obligations under this Agreement, the agency remains delinquent in meeting the most important, contained in Section 3, of accomplishing the reintroduction of the Mexican Wolf into the wild "as expeditiously as possible."
>
> Pursuant to Section 3 of the Agreement, the Service issued a Time line dated July 1, 1993 which called for a final Environmental Impact Statement and the release of Mexican wolves by March 1995. That was one year ago, and we still do not have a final EIS or any release of wolves.

The letter went on to express that the plaintiffs had been patient with the Service in this effort and wished to remain "a constructive and supportive player in the recovery of the Mexican Wolf in the Southwest," but requested that Kaufman promptly provide a statement of how the Service planned to comply with the provisions of the agreement. Actually, Burnett's letter contained a slight discrepancy. March 1995 was the date for the final EIS, but July 1996 was the date given in the *Stipulated Settlement Agreement* for the wolves' release.

I attended a late April 1996 meeting of Will and Jan Holder's Horse Springs management team for their Anchor Ranch, located in the lower Blue Range Area. Their management team included other neighboring ranchers, AGFD and USFS representatives, and environmentalists like me. Karen and Clay Riggs, holistic ranchers from Willcox, participated regularly and encouraged other ranchers in their southeastern Arizona area to adopt holistic ranching methods.

Anchor Ranch consists of about three hundred acres of

private land and ten thousand acres of the Apache National Forest. The Holders apply a holistic approach to their livestock management and do not kill predators. With every decision they make, the land and its natural inhabitants come first. They focus on strict organic production that prohibits use of artificial steroids or hormones, antibiotics, or pesticides. They refuse to employ cattle prods when moving the herds. Although the Holders believe their cattle deserve humane treatment, they also make a commitment for predators to coexist.

They planned to market their predator-friendly product as Ervin's Natural Beef. The product was named after Ervin Hicks, father of Will's mother, Clarice, who had been widely known for his honesty and integrity. A growing market for organic products already existed, so adding beef was exciting to several health-oriented cooperatives. However, the meat must be federally licensed and a butchering facility must be available before they could commercially market their product. Another problem they faced was their remoteness from an urban area where markets existed. The Holders wanted to work out all the kinks in this program before they asked other ranchers to join them in a cooperative venture.

During May 1996, Parsons released a draft of the Proposed Rule for the Proposed Establishment of a Nonessential Experimental Population of the Mexican Gray Wolf in Arizona and New Mexico for review. This document permitted use of the nonessential-experimental classification of the ESA, allowing more flexibility in management than full protection provided.

In mid-August, with no response forthcoming from Burnett's April letter to Kaufman, he wrote to her again:

> On behalf of the plaintiffs ... I requested, by letter dated April 19, that your office provide us a statement in writing of how it intends to comply with the provisions of the *Stipulated Settlement Agreement*, dated May 21, 1993,

including a prompt publication of the final EIS and a Time line for the release of wolves. To date, almost four months later, you have not responded to our letter and request.

We desire to be supportive of your office in the recovery of the Mexican wolf, and sincerely hoped that further legal action to enforce the 1993 Agreement would not be necessary. Your continued delay in publishing the final EIS and the release of wolves is unwarranted and violates the 1993 Agreement. Please be advised, therefore, that we intend to file appropriate legal action to enforce the 1993 Agreement unless your office responds to our request of April 19 within fifteen days of this letter.

On the fifteenth day, a clerk in Director Kaufman's office called Attorney Burnett to inform him that Kaufman had received his letter. Burnett responded that this response would not be satisfactory to his clients.

I wrote a letter to David Mech about our grave concerns that continued delays in the reintroduction might have negative effects on the captive animals awaiting their freedom. I explained that I believed part of the reason for continued delays was pressure on the USFWS from residents in local rural communities who feared that reintroduction of wolves would be detrimental to their economy. Mech responded as chair of the International Union for Conservation of Nature's Wolf Specialist Group and said:

> You raise some excellent questions. Of course we cannot advise on political aspects of the reintroduction program. However, from a biological standpoint, we certainly agree that the sooner reintroduction can take place, the more successful it should be. Holding the wolves in captivity longer, especially years longer, not only would be expensive, but it also might make it more difficult for them to adapt to their new, wild environment. In addition, the longer they are held, the more controlled breeding management would be necessary to maintain the genetic integrity of the captive population. . . .

We also agree that wolves tend to have a new positive value to the public. The town of Ely, Minnesota, for example, has shown a $3,000,000 annual increase in its economy resulting from the International Wolf Center. Economist John Duffield predicted a $19 million annual net benefit of the wolves reintroduced to Yellowstone.

This letter was copied and widely circulated to politicians, ranchers, and wolf advocates. Because all letters to Secretary Babbitt concerning the Mexican wolf were forwarded to Parsons for him to review and then brief the Washington office on content and the number of letters, I contacted Jamie Clark, then director of ecological services, and asked her to hand-carry a copy of Mech's letter to Babbitt's desk. I asked the P.A.WS. members and members of other supporting groups to send e-mail or to phone the office of Secretary Babbitt, urging him to expedite the Mexican wolf reintroduction process.

In August 1996, Parsons reported that Kaufman had completed her review of the final EIS and would brief Secretary Babbitt on it before the end of the month. At the end of August, I contacted the Washington USFWS office to learn how the briefing had gone. Kaufman had delayed the briefing until mid-September. Late in September, I called Parsons to learn the outcome of the briefing only to be told that Director Kaufman had imposed a gag order on the entire Albuquerque staff, forbidding them to communicate in any fashion with any wolf advocates. This action was completely unprecedented. At that point, no formal legal action had been taken by our coalition of wolf advocate groups for the violations of the *Stipulated Settlement Agreement* of 1993.

On October 2, 1996, Burnett, on behalf of twenty-seven conservation groups, mailed a sixty-day notice of intent to sue for violation of the ESA to Babbitt. The letter pointed out the obligation of the USFWS to implement the Mexican Wolf Recovery Plan, which it had approved on September 15, 1982.

The Service has failed to implement the Recovery Plan, which calls for the establishment of a wild population within the Mexican Wolf's historic range, and thus has violated its duties. . . .

In addition, the Service's failure to implement the Recovery Plan for the Mexican Wolf violates the *Stipulated Settlement Agreement* dated May 21, 1993 and entered into by parties in the case of Wolf Action Group, et al. V. United States . . . The *Stipulated Settlement Agreement* imposed a number of duties on the Service in connection with the implementation of the Mexican Wolf Recovery Plan. The Service remains inexcusably delinquent in meeting the most important requirement, contained in Section 3, of accomplishing the reintroduction of the Mexican wolf into the wild "as expeditiously as possible" and in accordance with the Proposal and General Plan for an Experimental Release of the Mexican Wolf, dated February 19, 1991.

Pursuant to Section 3 of the Agreement, the Service issued a Time line dated July 1, 1993 which called for a final Environmental Impact Statement and the release of Mexican wolves by March, 1995. That was 18 months ago, and the Service still has not issued a final EIS or released any wolves. Further delay in publishing the final EIS and releasing wolves is not warranted.

Accordingly, please be advised that we intend to file appropriate legal action to compel compliance with the Endangered Species Act and the 1993 *Stipulated Settlement Agreement.*

During that year, when it seemed that we wolf advocates were trudging through endless mud, one event delighted us. We received news of the May birth of three Mexican wolf pups, two males and one female, to Rosa, the female at the Phoenix Zoo. These births, her firstborn pups, were welcomed by the captive management committee because Rosa possessed rare genetic characteristics beneficial to the captive population. Two of these pups later were released in the Blue Range Area.

Success Follows Many Delays

But ask the animals, and they will teach you, or birds of the air, and they will tell you; or speak to the earth and it will teach you, or let the fish of the sea inform you. Which of all these does not know that the hand of the Lord has done this? In his hand is the life of every creature and the breath of all mankind.
—Job 12: 7–10

Early in 1996, I decided that rather than giving educational wolf presentations in individual school classrooms, a much more efficient method of reaching larger numbers of school children would be for P.A.WS. to offer teachers' workshops. At these workshops we would educate teachers, and they, in turn, would provide information to their students. I contacted Beth Church, education and conservation director at Wolf Haven International, who had taken over this position after Paul Joslin left. Church and I augmented Wolf Haven's teachers' curriculum guide on wolves, which lacked information on the Mexican wolf. P.A.WS. financed the publication of fifteen hundred copies of this guide, which were later provided to teachers who attended our workshops. In addition, we produced a much needed educational brochure. P.A.WS. purchased three thousand copies of the brochures, which were distributed to educators and also used as handouts at our public outreach events, such as the Tempe Arts Festival.

I put together two large trunks full of educational items for teachers to use in the classroom. The trunks contained furs, plastic paw prints, and skulls of wolves, coyotes, bobcats, deer, and elk as well as many books, videos, and audiocassette tapes of wolf howls. These trunks would be loaned out to teachers who first participated in a three-hour workshop on wolves.

I enlisted the aid of a few interested P.A.WS. members, Meg Hendrick, Donna Storie, Wanda Winningham, and Jennifer Donovan, in addition to Phoenix Zoo staff members Karen Schedler and Joanne Kirchner. From fall 1996 through early 1998, we conducted about a dozen well-attended workshops in both Phoenix and Tucson. These workshops are now being conducted under the leadership of Karen Schedler, who later became the AGFD's environmental education program manager.

Later in 1996, Ted Turner offered to assist the USFWS with captive breeding of Mexican wolves by building a facility similar to Sevilleta on his Ladder Ranch, near Truth or Consequences, New Mexico. P.A.WS. member Jay Nochta volunteered to help with the construction for two weeks and ended up staying for the duration of the project, which took three and a half months. Nochta's willingness to work long hours whatever the difficulty of the job he was asked to do, plus his artistry in wood sculpture, made a big impression.

In December 1996, after several broken timelines, the final EIS for Mexican wolf reintroduction was published. David Parsons sent six copies to the offices of the Environmental Protection Agency (EPA). They, in turn, issued a notice to the Federal Register and published a notice of availability. At least thirty days had to elapse between the printing of this notice and the signing of a Record of Decision (ROD) by Interior Secretary Bruce Babbitt.

The signing of the ROD would alert the USFWS to print the Final Rule for the Proposed Establishment of a Nonessential Experimental Population of the Mexican Gray Wolf in Arizona and New Mexico. This final version would include resolutions to the many issues questioned in the draft of the Proposed Rule of 1996. The signing of the ROD also signaled the go-ahead for implementation for the reintroduction of the Mexican wolf.

During December, staff from the USFWS Albuquerque office scheduled a public meeting at their Phoenix office, both to announce the publication of and to distribute copies of the final EIS on the *Reintroduction of the Mexican Wolf Within Its Historic Range in the Southwestern United States*. I borrowed a box full of some fifteen thousand signatures gathered on petitions back in the early 1990s by the Mexican Wolf Coalition of New Mexico, and four thousand signatures gathered by the Lobo Restoration Project, a Texas wolf support group, and four thousand signatures gathered in Phoenix and Tucson by P.A.WS. members. I presented this large box of twenty-three thousand signatures to the USFWS staff presiding at the final EIS announcement gathering.

At that time twenty-nine cooperating breeding sites maintained a total of 149 Mexican gray wolves. Ten Mexican wolves had been transported to the Sevilleta National Wildlife Refuge compound from captive facilities in Missouri, New Mexico, Ohio, Michigan, Illinois, Minnesota, California, Texas, and Mexico. A USFWS wolf biologist, Colleen Buchanan, cared for these wolves. Buchanan earned her bachelor's degree in wildlife biology from New Mexico State University at Las Cruces in 1993. She had held student positions with the USFWS in Albuquerque during her years of study, and in January 1994 was given a permanent position in the regional office of planning. In May 1995, she became manager of the Sevilleta facility.

From an observation tower, she could monitor the five fenced areas on a daily basis, and she reported that the pairs appeared to be adapting very well. Each area was about one-third to one-half acre in size. She provided a minimum of human contact during the preconditioning period, before the wolves' eventual transfer to their acclimation pens in the Blue Range Area.

Late in February 1997, the sixty-day letter of intent to file a lawsuit had more than expired, and USFWS officials had taken no action to seek approval of the ROD. A phone conference took place among the principal plaintiffs: Defenders of Wildlife, Audubon, P.A.WS., the Southwest Center for Biodiversity, and Attorney Burnett. We resolved that we had no recourse but to proceed with the lawsuit.

During these political machinations, I kept asking myself, "Shouldn't the welfare of this endangered species be a top priority of the USFWS? Why should Mexican wolves have to languish away in captivity while officials within the D.C. beltway debate the effect the wolves' freedom might have on their political future?" A bond tied me to these wolves that I could not define. I could only feel it inside me just like I could feel my heart beating.

Dr. Robin Silver, cofounder of the Southwest Center for Biodiversity, a physician and professional photographer, produced, at his own expense, thousands of large full-color Mexican wolf posters for distribution. The poster's message urged calls to Interior Secretary Babbitt to expedite implementation of the Mexican Wolf Recovery Plan.

In an eleventh hour attempt to avoid legal action, Rodger Schlickeisen, president of Defenders, met with John Rogers, acting director of USFWS. He requested an explanation for the extended USFWS delays. Schlickeisen informed Rogers that the coalition of environmental groups that had filed the sixty-day letter of intent had completely run out of patience and were about to file a lawsuit if immediate action was not taken to obtain Secretary Babbitt's signature on the ROD, approving the USFWS-recommended Alternative A in the final EIS. According to Schlickeisen, Rogers was surprised and apologetic.

Schlickeisen later learned that the USFWS rationale for the delays was that the staff was being cautious. The ROD must have three signatures of approval, those of Secretary Babbitt, the secretary of defense (because of the White Sands connection), and the secretary of agriculture (because the release area is within two national forests administered by the Forest Service). Schlickeisen reported that the USFWS told him that the ROD process would move as fast as the bureaucracy allowed.

The primary plaintiffs considered the recent developments. Burnett had all the legal ammunition needed for the lawsuit, but we agreed that our filing could cause additional delays. It appeared that the signing of the ROD was very close, and Secretary Babbitt had given no indication that he was opposed to the reintroduction.

Schlickeisen's ultimatum apparently jolted Rogers and his immediate staff, who moved the final EIS and the ROD to the desk of Secretary Babbitt. On March 4, 1997, Secretary Babbitt signed the ROD, and the document was subsequently signed by Raymond J. Fatz, deputy assistant secretary of the army. Following Secretary Babbitt's approval, a nationwide burst of publicity exploded in newspapers and on television about this momentous event, even though the third signature had not been obtained. Editorials, including one on March 7, 1997, by Linda Valdez in the *Arizona Republic,* hailed the decision as the right one for the state of Arizona and the Southwest.

After several days, Dan Glickman, secretary of agriculture, still had not signed the ROD. All sorts of rumors evolved as to the cause of this delay. Were the Arizona and New Mexico Cattle Growers Associations pressuring him not to sign? Was Glickman miffed at the rash of publicity that preceded his signature?

On March 4, 1997, Arizona Governor Fife Symington wrote a letter to Glickman, in which he stated, "The State of Arizona does not believe the U.S. Fish and Wildlife Service has adequately addressed some very serious problems which may result from Mexican Gray wolf reintroduction into the State of Arizona in the near future." Governor Symington requested that

Secretary Glickman not sign the ROD. Symington concluded his letter by stating: "In closing, I would also like to point out that neither the Arizona Game and Fish Commission nor the U.S. Forest Service supported reintroduction of the Mexican Gray wolf into the State of Arizona."

This statement flew in the face of a January 22, 1997, letter from the AGF Commission, written by the then-chair Nonie Johnson to Nancy Kaufman, Region 2 director for the USFWS, confirming the Commission's support for the decision on the final EIS. While expressing the Commission's preference for an initial release in White Sands, she wrote, "We reiterate our position that, should the Service decide on wolf reintroduction in the Blue Range Area, we will diligently work with you to ensure that the effort has every reasonable opportunity for success, and that any impacts on other resources and the public are minimized to the fullest extent possible."

New Mexico Governor Gary Johnson wrote an urgent letter to Secretary Glickman similar to Symington's, asking Glickman not to approve the ROD.

I made emphatic phone calls to the secretary of agriculture's office to find out why Glickman had not signed the ROD. Their public relations official informed me that the only reason the secretary had not signed the final ROD was because he had been out of Washington, and had just returned on March 7. On Wednesday, March 12, the same official called me to relay the good news that Secretary Glickman had signed the ROD. The Mexican wolf reintroduction process had been given the green light.

At the May 1997 meeting of the Holder's Horse Springs management team for the Anchor Ranch, Will and Jan Holder announced that they were actively pursuing plans to market their predator-friendly product, Ervin's Natural Beef. Will and

Jan Holder had applied and been granted the proper USDA license. They spent months trying to find a butchering house that would process their beef and finally obtained an agreement with the University of Arizona's butchering facility. They actively solicited markets for Ervin's Natural Beef and were successful in finding several outlets. This enterprise meant sacrificing many hours away from the ranch, during which time they had to hire help to keep the ranch operating properly.

During that same month, Terry Johnson began working with Parsons to achieve a Memo of Understanding to define the specific role of the AGFD in the reintroduction process. This memo made it clear that the USFWS would provide a Mexican wolf recovery coordinator (David Parsons) to serve as the focal point for the Service on all matters involving wolf recovery, and a field biologist (Wendy Brown) to oversee wolf management activities. They would also help to fund a Mexican wolf biologist to be hired by AGFD to "coordinate and implement wolf reintroduction and management activities in Arizona and New Mexico for the Department." The Memo of Understanding was signed by AGFD Director Duane Shroufe on June 23, 1997, and by USFWS Region 2 Director Nancy Kaufman on July 3, 1997.

The total Mexican wolf population had climbed to 178, with thirty-six new pups born during 1997. At a July species survival plan meeting in Texas, where the 1998 breeding decisions were made, Alberto Aldamo, Mexican wolf biologist from Mexico, announced that their biologists planned to reintroduce Mexican wolves in Mexico.

In early June 1997, a site selection committee, headed by Wendy Brown, explored potential sites for the acclimation pens for the Mexican wolves. Other members of this committee included Mike Rising, from the Springerville USFS office; Jim Hinkle, from the AGFD office in Pinetop; Marty Moore, representing Apache County; and Steve Faraizl, of USDA Wildlife Services. Don Hoffman of the Alpine District Forest Service, while not an official member of this committee, provided valuable information on many of the sites considered.

While on my July 1997 summer camping trip to Luna Lake near Alpine, I learned that a few of the residents had been misinformed that a USFWS biologist would be implementing all day-to-day operations of the Mexican wolves in the Blue and conducting all interaction with the local community. I knew that this rumor ran contrary to the recently signed Memo of Understanding between the USFWS and AGFD, which stated that the Service would provide financial help for the salary of a wolf biologist who would work for the Department. Someone had convinced the local residents that the AGFD had abdicated their responsibility for the Mexican wolf project at their October 1995 Commission meeting, when they voted for a proposal recommending reintroduction at White Sands.

I tried to explain to the confused local residents that the only reason the Commission worded their proposal that way was to ensure a majority vote for the Department's future participation. If the Commission had recommended the Blue Range Area, the vote surely would have failed. This would have all but eliminated the AGFD from further participation in Mexican wolf recovery. Without Arizona's participation, it is doubtful that Parsons could have obtained Secretary Babbitt's approval to go ahead with the program.

When I returned to Phoenix, I had lunch with Terry Johnson; Jeff Williamson, executive director of the Phoenix Zoo; Bill Van Pelt, AGFD's endangered mammals program manager; and Mike Seidman, lead zoo keeper at the Phoenix Zoo. I reported on the rumors I'd heard from Alpine residents. None of them knew why anyone would seek to misinform the local people about future wolf activities. Johnson said that the Memo of Understanding stipulated that the new Department wolf biologist would be handling day-to-day wolf operations as well as local interaction. He said he would meet with the USFWS staff and clear the air on the roles the AGFD and USFWS would play in the reintroduction program.

During lunch, Williamson expressed concerns that the USFWS plans for the acclimation period called for the use of volunteers, but no one with training on how to handle wolves was mentioned in the plans. He offered to loan Seidman to supervise the volunteers during the acclimation period. Johnson was pleased by this offer and was sure Parsons would agree with this arrangement.

Following our luncheon discussion, Johnson scheduled a meeting in Pinetop on October 6, 1997, at which he and other AGFD staff as well as Parsons, Brown, and other USFWS staff would discuss their roles in the recovery program. Soon after the October 6 Pinetop meeting, Johnson told me, "Our discussions held were, in some cases, difficult, and what was said will remain within the confines of the meeting room. Those issues with which you are primarily concerned were all worked out satisfactorily." One of the things he could discuss with me was that those present agreed that there needed to be improved interaction among the several agencies and advocacy groups, so that all involved were kept up to date on current happenings.

The process for site selection begun in May 1997 dragged on. I had believed originally that the selection would be final by July and construction would be commencing in August 1997, but by October, final selection still had not been settled. Finally, in November, the selection was completed, with three sites designated for pen construction in 1997, and four other sites on the list for use in subsequent years. The initial three were Campbell Blue, Hawk's Nest, and Turkey Creek. The other four were

Crow Poison Spring, Engineer Spring, Pace Creek, and Triple X Ranch.

Steve Crozier, an Americorps volunteer assigned to the Mexican wolf recovery program, was to be in charge of the BRWRA pen construction, and was actively soliciting names of potential volunteers. A number of P.A.WS. members volunteered.

By then the high country was well into winter weather, so instead of starting the construction in August with balmy conditions, the volunteers had to brave snow and slush during their construction of the Mexican wolf acclimation pens. Crozier arranged for volunteers to work at the Campbell Blue and the Hawk's Nest pens. I later learned that Crozier, whose background included work as an accountant, had no experience in putting up ten-foot-high sections of heavy chain-link fence or in burying and stabilizing fence posts. Fortunately, Don Hoffman was loaned to the project for the construction of the first two pens, and as P.A.WS. member David Bluestein reported later, "It was truly beautiful to watch Don at work. He seemed to do everything so effortlessly." Both Bluestein and member Will Stefanov were surprised to see that these two pen sites were so close to State Route 191 and to Alpine.

By the time the Campbell Blue and Hawk's Nest pens were completed, Crozier had acquired enough experience to supervise construction of the Turkey Creek pen without assistance from Hoffman. The pens were completed in early January 1998, just in time for the initial transfer of Mexican wolves into Campbell Blue.

Late in 1997, Parsons's final version of the Nonessential Experimental Population Rule was still being reviewed in Albuquerque and had not reached the final critical reviews in the Washington office of USFWS. Both Terry Johnson and Bill Van Pelt expressed concern because Arizona would forbid entry into the state of the endangered wolves for transfer to the acclimation pens if this final version of the rule were not approved.

Plans being made for a late January 1998 wolf transfer would have to be delayed.

To make matters worse, rumors abounded that the New Mexico Cattle Growers Association, the New Mexico Farm Bureau, and other anti-wolf groups intended to initiate a lawsuit to prevent the imminent reintroduction of Mexican wolves.

The Big Event

We reached the old wolf in time to watch a fierce green fire dying in her eyes. I realized then, and have known ever since, that there was something new to me in those eyes—something known only to her and to the mountain. I was young then, and full of trigger-itch; I thought that because fewer wolves meant more deer, that no wolves would mean hunters' paradise. But after seeing the green fire die, I sensed that neither the wolf nor the mountain agreed with such a view.

—Aldo Leopold, *A Sand County Almanac*

I nearly jumped out of my skin a few weeks before the initial transfer of wolves when Terry Johnson called to tell me I had been selected to help carry one of the three crates. The initial placement would transfer a wolf pair and their yearling female youngster from Sevilleta into the Campbell Blue pen.

The date for the big event had to coincide with Interior Secretary Bruce Babbitt's schedule. He had asked to be present, as he jokingly said, "to take all the credit." The date was set for January 26, 1998. The Final Experimental Population Rule was published in the Federal Register just two weeks before the scheduled transfer of wolves.

Johnson arranged a ride for me to the event with Gary Shafer, who had been with the AGFD for thirteen years, first as a public relations specialist, and then as video specialist and producer. On January 25, I drove to the AGFD building in north Phoenix to meet Gary, and on arrival, he told me we would be joined by Jan White, Department veterinarian in charge of operations at the Adobe Mountain Wildlife Center. Staff at the

Department had learned at the eleventh hour that Wendy Brown, who was responsible for supplying a veterinarian for the event, had not done so. White had been notified just one day earlier and had flown back from Florida, where she had been studying birds that had been victims of offshore oil spills. She had been notified to get on the next flight and return for the wolf transfer.

The high country in the Blue was covered with two feet of snow when we arrived. The celebration started on the evening of January 25, with a reception at Hannagan Meadow Lodge. Several P.A.WS. members had driven up for the big event, and they were joined by Will and Jan Holder, who provided Ervin's Natural Beef for the evening buffet, which was sponsored by Defenders of Wildlife, who took charge of the program.

Rodger Schlickeisen presided at the evening program, which was attended by more than two hundred people. About half of them were from the media. Schlickeisen talked about Defenders's role in wolf reintroduction programs, and about the threat posed to the Yellowstone wolves by the recent lawsuit calling for their removal. He introduced Mike Phillips, project leader for the Yellowstone reintroduction, and told the media folks that Phillips could answer their questions about the threats to the Yellowstone wolves.

The AGFD had originally planned to host a small, informal reception for the principals involved with the Mexican wolf reintroduction, and their staff was not happy to have outsiders, only remotely connected with the implementation of the project, take over the evening. I heard some Arizona activists grumbling about the amount of emphasis placed on Yellowstone wolves at our Mexican wolf celebration.

Following his remarks, Schlickeisen introduced Interior Secretary Bruce Babbitt, who returned the focus of the evening to the accomplishments of local wolf advocates in bringing back el lobo to the Blue. Although a former Arizona rancher himself, Secretary Babbitt spoke exuberantly of the wolves' return.

I shared a cabin at Hannagan Meadow Lodge with Mike Golightly, AGF commissioner, and his wife, Susan. We had an opportunity to talk about our hopes for the reintroduction program's future and the actual release of the wolves into the forest.

A horse trailer carrying the family of three Mexican wolves in three steel crates was parked overnight outside our cabin. Biologists ensured their well-being before we all retired. I tossed and turned like a kid before Christmas day, knowing that within a few feet of my bed, outside my cabin window, were the first Mexican wolves ever to set foot on Blue Range ground for over half a century. On nearby Escudilla Mountain, Aldo Leopold had shot that green-eyed female wolf made famous in his *Sand County Almanac*. Now just fifty years after her death in 1948, we were about to return Mexican wolves to their rightful habitat. Had we finally learned the meaning of Leopold's essay "Thinking Like a Mountain"? I lay there listening to the wolves periodically howl and thrash about and did not sleep the entire night.

Early on the morning of Monday, January 26, a large crowd gathered outside the lodge in the snow under sunny skies, awaiting the arrival of Secretary Babbitt for a brief ceremony. He gave an eloquent speech, expressing his joy for the return of the Mexican wolf, but stressing the importance of all of us working together with the local communities to ensure that the reintroduction would be successful. Kate Hunger, in Tucson's *Arizona Daily Sun*, quoted Babbitt saying, "These wolves, if they're managed properly, can be pretty good neighbors. There's room enough and space enough in God's creation that we can all live in harmony on this landscape."

The Campbell Blue acclimation pen was about five miles

southeast of Alpine. Those permitted to attend the actual transfer of the wolves from their crates into the pens were first shuttled five miles in successive groups in vans, and then one mile and a half in snow cats to a quarter mile from the pen site. Attendees walked the remaining distance. Observers were held behind yellow rope about fifty feet from the pen.

The crate carriers were the last to arrive, with USFWS biologists on snow cats carrying the crated wolves. An awed hush fell over the crowd of eighty-some people scattered under the ponderosa pines near the wolf acclimation pen. The crate carriers carefully carried the three steel crates inside the pen and gently set them down in the snow.

Interior Secretary Bruce Babbitt pulled the first crate door of the alpha female wolf, #174. Duane Shroufe, director of the AGFD, pulled open the second crate door, and ten-month-old female wolf #511 burst from the crate to race about the one-third acre snow-covered pen. She stopped and looked back at the many photographers and television camera crew watching her. Then she explored her new surroundings and was joined instantly by her mother, #174. The two wolves frolicked in the snow under sunny skies as the onlookers sighed, smiled, and shared a few meaningful hugs. I could not hold back the tears that filled my eyes.

I was assigned to open the door of the third crate, and it slid easily up and out of its grooves. It was hard to contain my exhilaration. The adult alpha male wolf, #166, in the third crate faced backwards and was reluctant to leave. He remained there until after the crate carriers and observers had left the area. We four carriers of crate three were later teased as to why our wolf would not leave his crate. Biologists who remained reported that after about one hour, the male wolf walked out of his crate and sniffed the surrounding air with uncertainty until he saw his family. Then he bounded over to mother and daughter, and a happy family reunion with whimpers, licks, and waggly tails ensued. Mike Phillips told me, "Don't worry, Bobbie, the more cautious wolves are the ones that are most likely to survive in the wild."

Other carriers of the wolf crates were, on the first crate, Jamie Clark, current director of the USFWS; Trish Stevenson, granddaughter of Aldo Leopold, representing their family; and Will Holder, rancher from Anchor Ranch. On the second crate were Jose Luis Samaniego Leyva, coordinator of internal affairs, Ministry of Environment in Mexico; Nancy Kaufman, Region 2 director for the USFWS; and Rodger Schlickeisen, president of Defenders of Wildlife. On the third crate were John Kirkpatrick, acting director for Region 3 of the USFS; David Henderson, Southwest representative for the Audubon Society; and Kent Newton, assistant director of the Albuquerque Biological Park.

Following the release of the three wolves into the Campbell Blue pen, the crowd made its way back to where the snow cats picked them up. It took well over an hour to walk that one-quarter mile because of the many media people who blocked the path as they flocked around Secretary Babbitt and other dignitaries with their cameras and note pads. Babbitt again expressed his joy at the return of the Mexican wolves, saying to Patrick O'Driscoll of *USA Today,* "As we bring these wolves back to the wild, we strengthen the human spirit." "Today we are putting the green fire back on the mountain," said Jamie Clark to Carla McClain of the *Tucson Citizen.*

When interviewed by Steve Bodinet of Phoenix TV channel 3 about my reaction to the return of the wolves, I exclaimed, "I am elated! I just want to take this moment and freeze it in time."

Terry Johnson echoed my sentiments when he responded to Bodinet, "It was truly magnificent. It's rewarding to be present to see the first Mexican wolves set foot on the ground here in the Blue."

I was surprised to see Barbara Marks, rancher and outspoken opponent of wolves, on the incline. She told Steve Yozwiak of the *Arizona Republic,* "That certainly wasn't an animal that's afraid of man, which concerns me greatly." She told Carla McClain of the *Tucson Citizen,* "I am not too tickled about it, to say the least. I'm here, but not because I favor it." But Marks accepted one of the commemorative wolf T-shirts being given to attendees by the AGFD.

As reported by Keith Bagwell in the *Arizona Daily Star,* another rancher present, Hugh McKeen from Catron Country in New Mexico, said, "It's the worst thing that could happen to us. I have no doubt the wolves will be a problem for my cows. They will take down the first thing they come upon."

In his January 27 article, Bagwell went on to admit that not all ranchers present were opposed. Will and Jan Holder expressed their excitement about having the Mexican wolf returned to the forest. "I'm excited as hell!" Will exclaimed. "I've heard the howl of a wolf is really something. It'll be neat to hear that. I'm waiting for it." Holder explained how with his grazing management, he has his cattle avoiding predator-prone areas, and that he no longer kills any predators. He said he would "stay one step ahead of them," referring to the arrival of wolves.

It was rewarding to know that there was such widespread interest in the return of the Mexican wolf. However, for the sake of the wolves, I agreed with the original planners of AGFD that TV footage by their media production staff could have been pooled out to all of the major networks on State Route 191. Press interviews could have been conducted elsewhere. This would have eliminated the media crush at the site, a result of so many major network camera people and nationwide press writers present. More than half of the crowd had never participated in the reintroduction process, but P.A.WS. members who had devoted hours of hard work were excluded from the pen site.

At the same time the big event was taking place at Campbell Blue, a small, poorly attended protest by local ranchers was taking place in the center of Alpine. Slogans on placards announced their reaction to the reintroduction: "Hello Wolf, Goodbye Hunting," "The wolf can't be reintroduced in D.C. because he is already in the White House," and "Don't Import Wolves, Deport Environmentalists." David "Dink" Robarts, who organized the protest, expressed his fury over the reintroduction. As reported by Kit Minclier of the *Denver Post,* Robarts said, "We believe they are a ploy or a tool to limit our access to public lands. Wolf lovers worship the created, not the Creator.... We believe the wolf was created by God and wasn't intended to be set aside and worshiped in a pagan manner. They hold wolves in higher esteem than their fellow man." The protestors claimed that they were the endangered species.

Johnson had asked me before the big event if I would like to stay over until Tuesday, January 27, the day following the actual transfer, to relax and savor the moment. He asked Parsons to join us for dinner that night, but Parsons declined. Johnson and I enjoyed a relaxing dinner at the well-known Bear Wallow Cafe in Alpine and reviewed the momentous day's happenings from the early morning snow cat ride to the actual placement of the first Mexican wolves on the ground in the Campbell Blue pen, from which they would be released to run free in the forest.

On the drive home on Tuesday, I asked Johnson who the new AGFD wolf biologist was to be, having heard that a decision had been made. He surprised me when he said, "Diane Boyd."

"How did you ever manage that?" I exclaimed. "She could have landed a much higher-paying job for someone like David Mech."

"Well, she'd just completed her doctorate at the University of Montana and was looking for a challenge."

"She'll have one here all right. From what I've read of Diane Boyd, she can make this work if anyone can."

We discussed how Boyd's worldwide background, year of

hands-on experiences with wolves, and credibility in the wolf world for her many articles published in scientific journals would benefit the future of the Mexican wolf reintroduction program.

I asked Johnson why Wendy Brown had felt it unnecessary to assign a vet for the transfer activity. "I asked her the same question," he answered. "She said that she never had a vet present when they transferred wolves into the pens at Sevilleta, and she didn't think a vet would be needed here." I found this appalling. Johnson assured me that the Department had already made arrangements for a vet from Pinetop to be present for future wolf transfers.

The ride home was one of those times when you just want to exclaim, "God's in His Heaven; all's right with the world." The early morning sun spilled its rays through the spruce and pine branches to splash on the white carpet of snow. We'd just successfully placed the first Mexican wolves back on their native ground in the Blue after fifty years of no wolves in the area. I'd been chosen to help carry and open one of the crates, and here I was having the rare opportunity to share an in-depth discussion with Terry Johnson, the chief architect for the reintroduction.

A few days later, a pair of Mexican wolves was transferred from the Sevilleta to the Turkey Creek pen, about fifty miles southeast of Alpine, and the day after, six Mexican wolves, a pair and their offspring, were transferred from the Wolf Haven International facility in Tenino, Washington, to the Hawk's Nest pen, about five miles southwest of Alpine.

The Mexican wolves had come back to the Blue.

A Prayer Answered and Bad Happenings

When, from the prisons of our cities, we look out to wilderness,
when we reach intellectually for such abstractions as the privilege
of leading a life . . . of integrity—I think we can turn to wolves. We
do sense in them courage, stamina, and a straightforwardness of
living; we do sense that they are somehow correct in the universe
and we are somehow still at odds with it.
—Barry Lopez, *Of Wolves and Men*

When he told me of Diane Boyd's acceptance of the position of
wolf biologist for the Mexican wolf reintroduction project, Terry
Johnson said he was overjoyed because her firsthand knowledge and field experience with wolves would lend a tremendous amount of stability to the entire recovery project. Widely
known for her years of working directly with wolves in both
Minnesota and Montana, Boyd was truly an answer to P.A.WS.'s
prayers because she would take charge of the day-to-day operations with our Mexican wolves. I soon learned that she had
married Ed Heger, her long-time friend from Montana, and her
last name was now Boyd-Heger. Ed had recently retired and
joined her in Alpine to help with her challenging activities.

For more than twenty years, Boyd-Heger had studied elu-
sive wildlife species and resolved sensitive problems in field
situations. She had lived in a remote area near Glacier National
Park, Montana, in rustic conditions for seventeen years. She also
had experience with wildlife abroad and had established field
protocol for a wolf research project in Romania.

If you have read such wolf books as Rick McIntyre's *A Society of Wolves* or *War Against the Wolf,* you are already aware of Boyd-Heger's exciting wolf adventures. After obtaining her bachelor's degree in wildlife management at the University of Minnesota, she worked for David Mech. Later, at the University of Montana, where she earned both her master's and doctorate degrees in wildlife ecology, she worked on Dr. Robert Ream's Wolf Ecology Project.

Boyd-Heger had worked closely with local livestock growers and game wardens to settle wildlife-human conflicts. In Alpine, she would undoubtedly be called upon to resolve similar issues.

Steve Rutz, an Americorps member under temporary assignment to USFWS, requested names of volunteers to spend time at an acclimation pen, assisting those assigned to work during the entire acclimation period. Seven P.A.WS. members volunteered their services during the nine-week period. Mike Seidman instructed the volunteers in acclimation protocol, and Diane Boyd-Heger and Paul Morey supervised their daily activities. Boyd-Heger wanted to minimize human interface with the wolves, so food and water was carried in as needed, but the workers did not spend time in the pens.

Paul Morey was hired by the USFWS as a biological technician, to work with Diane Boyd-Heger at the three Mexican wolf pens during the acclimation period. Born and raised in New Hampshire, Morey had worked as a biological technician on many projects prior to his appointment as head biotech on the Mexican wolf project. These projects include working at the USFS Redwood Sciences Lab in Northern California, where he surveyed for forest carnivores. He received his bachelor's in wildlife management from Humboldt State University in Arcata, California, in 1997.

An interagency field team, appointed by David Parsons to oversee project implementation, consisted of Wendy Brown, USFWS wildlife biologist in Albuquerque; Boyd-Heger, living in

Alpine with her husband, Ed; and Alan Armistead, Mexican wolf specialist of the USDA Wildlife Services, living in Springerville. Armistead would be responsible for examining any cases of wolf depredation and interacting with the local ranchers on such incidents.

P.A.WS. members who participated in "pen sitting" reported that although it was extremely cold, the excitement of being so close to the Mexican wolves and assisting with their care more than made up for the discomfort. "We went out and brought in road-killed elk for the wolves, and it was a tough and bloody job. But helping to care for these wolves was a real highlight of my life," Gary Wheat told P.A.WS. members at a March meeting after his experiences. Will Stefanov echoed Wheat's sentiments: "When we fed the wolves, and I had a chance to actually look into the eyes of a Mexican wolf, I knew that this was probably the closest I would ever be to a wild wolf. It was as though for just an instant something clicked between me and the wolf. It was a moment I'll treasure always."

This was indeed an exhilarating time for all P.A.WS. members, and naturally everyone wanted to know when the wolves would be released into the wild. David Parsons was evasive about naming a date, saying only that the release would occur during the first two weeks of April, and he made it clear that this would not be a public event.

Parsons finalized a Public Interaction Plan that was incorporated into a Mexican Wolf Interagency Management Plan that he had approved. He appointed an Interagency Management Advisory Group consisting of representatives of affected agencies and counties, including representatives from the White Mountain and San Carlos Apache Tribes.

On March 25, several anti-wolf groups, including the New Mexico Farm Bureau, New Mexico Cattle Growers Association, and Greenlee County Cattle Growers Association of Arizona, filed a lawsuit with the U.S. District Court in New Mexico against

Bruce Babbitt, secretary of the interior; Jeff Haskett, director of the USFWS *(this position was actually held by Jamie Clark)*; and Nancy Kaufman, USFWS Region 2 director, seeking to prevent the release of the Mexican wolves. The plaintiffs alleged that the defendants violated the National Environmental Policy Act (NEPA) and Administrative Procedure Act of the ESA with their decision to reintroduce Mexican gray wolves into the BRWRA. The lawsuit listed Karen Budd-Falen of Budd-Falen Law Offices as attorney for the plaintiffs, assisted by Lee Peters of Huber and Hernandez (U.S. District Court for the District of New Mexico, 1998).

The lawsuit charged that Mexican gray wolves already inhabited parts of Arizona and New Mexico (p. 9). The alleged violations included the following: The EIS ignored the customs and culture of the local area; the EIS is in violation of the NEPA and the ESA; defendants' determination to release animals that are dog-wolf or dog-coyote hybrids violates the Administrative Procedures Act and the ESA; and failure to ensure that the action did not jeopardize existence of other endangered or threatened species violates the ESA (pp. 11–19).

The allegations reflected Dennis Parker's earlier theories, contained in his widely distributed paper *Reintroduction of the Mexican Wolf: Instrument of Recovery or Instrument of Demise?* Based on the allegations, the plaintiffs asked the court to "enjoin Defendants from releasing any of these animals alleged to be Mexican wolves in the states of New Mexico or Arizona."

On March 27, 28, and 29 of 1998, P.A.WS. participated in our last Tempe Arts Festival, at which we had operated a booth since 1989. Black foreboding clouds dumped cold rain on Tempe, soaking our booth and the sixteen faithful volunteers who showed up for four-hour periods to help me with outreach and merchandise sales. Nasty weather the entire weekend nearly curtailed the event, but we stuck it out with fair results.

When I returned home on the evening of March 29, I had a call from Terry Johnson telling me that all eleven wolves had been released in the Blue that day, during a blizzard. "I was not present," said Johnson. I could tell by the tone of his voice that even though he was pleased by the wolves' release, he was devastated to have been omitted. Previously, he and Parsons had agreed that the release would take place on April 1 or 2. Subsequently, Johnson had made a family commitment for March 29. He told me that he had asked Parsons to allow my presence at the release but was refused. I was honored that he had made the request.

I found it hard to understand why the release had been scheduled on a day when Johnson would be unable to be present. Johnson had been the key person working on the Mexican wolf project for more than sixteen years, longer than anyone else connected with the project. Johnson is one tough nut to crack, and during the more than twelve years I have known him, I have never known of anything that so devastated him as being left out of the wolves' release. While I was thrilled that Mexican wolves were now roaming free in the forest, I was so disturbed by his omission from this happening that I wrote a letter of complaint about Parsons's decision to alter the release date to Jamie Clark, director of USFWS, copying both Parsons and Johnson.

I learned from staff at the AGFD Phoenix office that they were not happy when they learned of the March 29 release done without their knowledge. However, after a few days, officials at the Department decided that because continued cooperation between the two agencies was essential to the continued success of the program, they would drop their anger and accept Parsons's decision.

In a memo to Director Clark, Parsons wrote that he had released the wolves on March 29 to ensure their welfare, and he denied my accusations, saying my letter contained factual

errors. Johnson told me by phone that I had made a few tacti-
cal, not factual, errors in my letter to Jamie Clark, but my relating of the principal facts was right on. In a subsequent personal
letter, he thanked me for things I had said in my letter to Jamie
Clark about his role in bringing wolves back to the Southwest. Johnson asked me to drop the whole matter, because it
was imperative to work with USFWS staff to ensure the future
of our Mexican wolves. I followed his request. As he laughingly
said at the time, "It can all come out in your book."

The good news was that the wolves were running free, and
certainly their welfare was far more important than my rage
over the exclusion of Johnson from the release.

Processing of the New Mexico Farm Bureau's lawsuit took
several days, and it was not received by the USFWS until well
after the wolves had been released. Within a week of the filing
of this lawsuit, Defenders of Wildlife, joined by twelve other
conservation organizations and individuals, including P.A.WS.,
Sierra Club, Arizona League of Conservation Voters, and Southwest Center for Biodiversity, immediately sought to intervene
on behalf of the defendants. Grove Burnett, attorney from the
Western Environmental Law Center in Taos, New Mexico, famil-
iar with legal issues of the Mexican wolf recovery program, represented the intervenors' action. Defenders et al. delayed filing
their answer to the plaintiff's lawsuit until late June, the same
time that the USFWS filed their answer. The USFWS-published
review of Parker's controversial paper provided the defendants'
attorneys with scientific defense to refute the plaintiffs' claims.

In the May 1998 issue of *PAW PRINTS,* I announced to the members that now that Mexican wolves were back on the ground,
P.A.WS. would disband that August. Our goal to return the Mexican wolves to the wild had been accomplished; field biologists
and law enforcement officers must conduct future work for the
Mexican wolf. Some members expressed disappointment, but

most understood that after eleven years, we should not perpet-
uate the organization purely for social reasons.

P.A.WS.'s overall membership had grown to more than five
hundred members throughout the United States, Canada, and
twenty other countries. Through the years, a group of Phoenix
P.A.WS. members had served as the core for most of our volunteer activity. In addition to members helping at craft fairs and
art festivals and at educational and howling workshops, we
had the benefit of many fine speakers at our monthly meetings,
held from September through May of each year. Many of these
speakers were prominent in their fields, such as Rick McIntyre,
wildlife photojournalist; Luigi Boitani, wolf biologist from Italy;
Terry Johnson, AGFD's nongame branch chief; Hank Fischer,
northwest Rocky Mountain representative for Defenders of Wildlife; Joni Bosh, former national chair for the Sierra Club; Warren
Parker, former coordinator for the red wolf recovery program;
David Parsons, coordinator for the Mexican wolf recovery program; Suzanne Pfister, vice president in charge of public relations
for Nelson, Robb, DuVall and DeMenna; Warren Iliff, former
executive director of the Phoenix Zoo; Jeff Williamson, executive director of the Phoenix Zoo; Dick George, author, photojournalist, and director of publications for the Phoenix Zoo;
and Anne Coe, wildlife artist.

At our final meeting, Diane Boyd-Heger described her doctorate studies and experiences in the northern Rockies and
brought us up to date on the status of the released Mexican
wolves. This last meeting was held at the Camelback moun-
tainside home of Barbara Boltz, with a potluck dinner followed
by the program. The warm May evening carried an air of celebration, and I was honored to be presented several gifts from
dedicated P.A.WS. members.

12

No One Said It Would Be Easy

Nowadays it is not the wolf that is dangerous to man, but man that is dangerous to the wolf.

—Eric Zimen, *The Wolf*

All wolves from the three family groups soon left their pens to explore their new forested surroundings after the March 29 release. Despite wet and blustery winter weather, ground crews and AGFD aircraft tracked them with radio telemetry. The Campbell Blue pair appeared to be the most adventurous; they were located over two miles south of their pen in a large snow-covered open meadow. The gates on the three pens were closed within a week of their release, as the wolves demonstrated that they no longer needed the security of their acclimation pens. Diane Boyd-Heger reported, "Because the wolves are constantly on the move exploring their new territories, it's difficult for us to figure out the best location at which to leave road kill for the wolves to eat."

The Campbell Blue family continued to move the farthest to explore their area, which consists of gently rolling hills and open stands of ponderosa pine and small meadows. Although the trackers observed many elk, they didn't observe any elk kills during the early days of freedom. Supplemental feeding continued.

On Tuesday, April 4, 1998, Paul Morey observed the Hawk's Nest pack pursuing an adult elk. On that same day, a local resident reported that he saw wolves killing an elk in the Hawk's Nest territory. Diane Boyd-Heger inspected the carcass and found it to be a cow elk. She removed a jawbone for analysis of the elk's physical condition. Her analysis confirmed deterioration. She left the carcass alone for many days to allow the wolves to devour the rest of it. She told me, "The three wolves who had killed the elk were one of the yearling females and the two male pups. They remained nearby while I was examining the carcass." During a telemetry flight on April 22, she observed all five of the Hawk's Nest wolves feeding on the kill.

Federal and state agency personnel and wolf advocates hailed this event as a cause for celebration, because despite predictions to the contrary, captive-reared wolves had demonstrated their inherent ability to bring down a large game animal and provide food for themselves.

In early April, a mountain lion hunter, Corwin Estes of Eagar, camped two miles north of the Turkey Creek wolf-release pen. Jim Erickson reported in his May 1, 1998, article in the *Arizona Daily Star* that Estes told him, "Two wolves started coming around our camp four or five nights in a row when I fed my hounds. I threw my feeding bucket at them to drive them off, but they wouldn't leave." Estes believed that the wolves were hungry and added, "We moved camp in the middle of a hunt to get away from them because I was afraid they would attack my dogs. They were just a nuisance."

Another unnamed camper later reported that he previously had camped in the same spot with about thirty people and admitted that the group had thrown out leftover eggs from breakfast. The wolves appeared about one hundred feet away and fed on the discarded food. The wolves returned repeatedly looking for more food.

On April 28, less than a month after the wolves' release, Richard Humphrey, a camper whose camp was located in the same area, about a mile from the acclimation pen, well within the wolves' territory, shot and killed the four-year-old male Turkey Creek wolf, #156. According to information obtained later in the investigative report, Humphrey first reported to AGFD officials that the wolf had been fighting with his dog.

Upon learning of the wolf kill, Alpine project personnel immediately drove to the Turkey Creek site, where they were joined by law enforcement officials from the USFWS. Once these officials had started their investigation, a gag order was placed on all communications with the public concerning the killing.

The wolf's body was frozen and shipped to the USFWS forensic lab in Ashland, Oregon, for a necropsy. I anticipated that following the investigation, the U.S. Attorney in Arizona would prosecute the wolf killer.

The Report of Investigation on this incident was completed on May 6, 1998. Members of the public were required to request copies of the report by a letter citing provisions of the Freedom of Information Act. Results of the investigation infuriated me and hundreds of other wolf advocates; the USFWS investigative team released Richard Humphrey from any prosecution after he changed his story to say the wolf was threatening his family.

The investigative report revealed that Humphrey had changed his story following the initial report given to an AGFD official on April 28, 1998. In the initial report taken by AGFD Officer J. L. Shelton, which became part of the Report of Investigation, Humphrey, referred to as "RP," stated that the wolf attacked his dog. "When the RP tried to get the wolf off the dog it would not so he had to shoot one of the wolves in the gut. The other wolf ran off. The wolf that was injured only went a short distance and the RP shot it again killing it" (Insert 3, p. 12).

Following the incident, G.J. Sagi of the Safari Club International gave Richard Humphrey advice. It did not take a stroke of genius for them to consult the ESA and find the clause that would set Humphrey free:

Notwithstanding any other provision of this Act, it shall
be a defense to prosecution under this subsection if the
defendant committed the offense based on a good faith
belief that he was acting to protect himself or herself, a
member of his or her family, or any other individual, from
bodily harm from any endangered or threatened species.
(p. 39)

Mike Taugher reported the story Humphrey developed about
the wolf attack in the *Albuquerque Journal* on Wednesday, June
17, 1998. Humphrey said he killed the wolf during an April
camping trip because his family was in danger and he felt
threatened. "It was coming directly towards us ... It was
aggressive." He and Sagi made the rounds to several Tucson
television stations to be interviewed on his "life-threatening"
experience.

Obvious discrepancies existed between Humphrey's tale and
the veterinary medical examination report written by Richard
Stroud, veterinary medical examiner for the federal government's National Fish and Wildlife Forensics Laboratory in Ashland, Oregon. In the initial report, Humphrey had said that he
shot the wolf "in the gut" when it attacked his dog. It wasn't
until later, when providing his narrative to the federal investigators, that Humphrey changed this to claim, "I felt threatened." He said that he had a feeling that "the wolf had attacked
us" (Insert 3, p. 2).

The forensic medical report stated, "Wound track #1 pene-
trates both hind legs.... The wounds to the rear are in my
opinion the result of a single bullet passing through the left leg
just above the knee and continuing through the right leg....
The wolf would have to be standing with both feet together
directly broadside to the shooter to obtain this alignment of
the wounds" (Insert 16, p. 10). Would an attacking wolf have
been standing broadside?

Humphrey claimed that after the first shot, the wolf moved

about twenty feet away before the second shot. USFWS law enforcement staff claimed they saw a blood trail proving that the wolf moved (Insert 3, p. 4). There was speculation that the blood may have been from the wounded dog, because possibility of the wolf moving after the first shot was contradicted by the medical report, which stated, "The wound (1st shot) would, in my opinion, drop the rear of the animal and would have not permitted the animal to move unless he dragged his body using his front legs only. This would have resulted in contamination of the wounds to the hind legs with dirt. No evidence of wound contamination or dragging was evident" (Insert 16, p. 10).

Humphrey further claimed that his second shot was from a distance of about fifteen yards. The medical report stated that, "The wound track extends slightly diagonally and downward across the anterior chest." (Insert 16, p. 8.) Could a shot from fifteen yards away have had a downward angle?

Reportedly, it was after Richard Humphrey cited the clause from the ESA and related his frightening experience that the USFWS investigative team decided not to prosecute.

The decision to let Richard Humphrey off scot-free without even so much as a fine indicated that wolf advocates might have misplaced their trust in an agency that would allow this flawed decision to stand. It appeared to many of us that we could no longer look to the USFWS law enforcement personnel to provide justice for violations of the ESA. Carla McClain reported in the *Tucson Citizen* on June 16, 1998, that Nancy Zierenburg of the Tucson-based Wildlife Damage Review said, "They have doomed this wolf recovery to failure, and I blame Fish and Wildlife for it." The USFWS decision sent a clear message to others who opposed the wolf's return—"Go shoot a wolf and then claim it threatened a family member—you won't even be fined!"

P.A.WS. initiated a massive letter-writing campaign to Nancy Kaufman, Region 2 director of USFWS, asking for removal of these law enforcement officers who were unwilling to bring to justice the killer of an endangered species they are mandated to protect. The letters were never acknowledged nor was the case reopened when medical evidence revealed discrepancies in the testimony.

The lone female wolf #128, mate of the dead male, could not survive on her own, and Diane Boyd-Heger suspected the wolf might be pregnant. The female was recaptured and returned to the Sevilleta National Wildlife Refuge facility. On May 5, the female did give birth to one pup that survived only a few weeks before dying. The female was probably too thoroughly traumatized and drugged during recapture to be capable of a healthy birth. While thin upon her return to Sevilleta, she later recovered but would not be considered as a candidate for a future release.

The shooting of the Turkey Creek male wolf alerted the Mexican wolf project personnel to the need for posting signs indicating to the public that they were in wolf country. Project staff posted large informative wolf recovery signs along strategic routes, where campers and local people would observe them, both in town and along State Route 191. In addition, the staff established several educational kiosks at strategic locations, providing protocol to minimize wolf-human conflicts for the public to observe while traveling and camping in wolf country.

About mid-May, Boyd-Heger told me on the phone that she thought both the Hawk's Nest and Campbell Blue alpha females had given birth to pups. Their movements were limited and denning was indicated. Both areas were closed to the public within a mile radius of the denning area, in which the wolves remained.

Shortly after this, Boyd-Heger reported that two young females, one from each pack, had dispersed from their packs' areas. The Hawk's Nest female #494 spent several days in and near Alpine. The Campbell Blue female #511 was first seen by children on a school bus, running along the highway, heading toward Springerville. Female wolf #511 had become known as the "poster wolf" because of the excellent pictures taken of her on January 26, 1998, one of which was blown up into a poster and widely distributed by the AGFD.

Biologists believed that while such dispersal patterns were perfectly natural for young wolves seeking mates, no wolf mates were available in the area. Not wanting to wait until either wolf was harmed or became involved in activities harmful to the success of the recovery program, they decided to live capture the two females and return them to Sevilleta.

Biologists began efforts to recapture female wolf #511. She approached a cow and a calf, and biologists tracking her from an airplane scared her away. For a time she appeared to be heading back into the wolf recovery area, but on May 13, she was spotted again well outside the boundary. On May 16, she wounded a miniature horse colt owned by Edwin Marsh of Heber. After examining the colt's wounds, wildlife specialist Alan Armistead said that the colt suffered puncture wounds on its neck consistent with a canid attack. Craig Miller of Defenders of Wildlife promised compensation for veterinary treatment of the colt. Female wolf #511 then traveled to Linden, northwest of Show Low, a distance of some seventy miles.

On Monday, May 18, female wolf #511 was netted. Tom Jackson King, a reporter at the time for the *White Mountain Independent,* was attempting to get the latest status update of the wandering wolf. *The Independent* is distributed twice weekly, on Tuesdays and Fridays. King had a 9:00 A.M. deadline for an article on the wolf that would appear as the headline story the next day. Bruce Sitko, information and education coordinator for the AGFD's Region 1 office, had communicated with King for more than two hours on Friday regarding the status of the wolf, wolf behavior, and the actions of the Mexican wolf project personnel in their efforts to capture wolf #511.

Regarding the incident, Sitko told me, "During our conversations, King repeatedly stated his concern over the proximity of the wolf to local communities and what he believed to be potential for an attack on people. I informed him of the lack of any documented attacks on humans by wolves, and said that if the Department thought there was any reason for concern of public safety, that we would be attempting to destroy the wolf at this moment rather than monitoring it until we had the proper equipment for a capture."

As King's deadline approached on Monday, he and Sitko spoke again by phone. Sitko said of the conversation, "I told him we had a jet helicopter, with greater maneuvering power, in the air at that very minute with a well-trained, experienced net gunner that had come in over the weekend from our Yuma office. However, we had not yet captured the wolf and had nothing new to report at that time."

King submitted his story. In it, he wrote that the wolf was indeed a threat to public safety, despite what Sitko had told him, quoting a Navajo County deputy sheriff as advising all local residents to keep their children and pets indoors until the wolf was caught. By 11:00 A.M. Monday morning, the wolf had been captured with the net gun and was on her way back to Sevilleta. When the story in the *Independent* hit the newsstands on Tuesday, May 19, and Sitko realized what King had written, along with the potential for resulting public hysteria, Sitko made a concerted effort that day to go immediately on local radio stations with information that the wolf had been captured and that there was never any cause for public alarm.

On May 18, Parsons, who had watched the capture from a low-flying helicopter as a net gunner worked for two hours to net her, remarked to Taugher of the *Albuquerque Journal,* "She had tremendous stamina. I couldn't believe her excellent condition after her long journey." When she was returned to Sevilleta, Colleen Buchanan reported to Taugher that the wolf was exceptionally large and healthy and "acting much wilder than before her release to the wild."

The Hawk's Nest female #494 continued her stay in and near Alpine. Boyd-Heger was receiving round-the-clock complaints from alarmed residents about the ranging female wolf. This wolf was finally captured by project personnel in a rubber-padded trap near Alpine after twenty-one days of interacting with horses and cattle and having been frequently observed by local residents. While she never harmed any animal or human during her wanderings, her continued presence in a human-populated area was upsetting the local people. Boyd-Heger reported, "The monitoring and capture of this wolf has been a great team effort. It could not have been accomplished without the cooperation of local residents."

Female wolf #494 was returned to Sevilleta on May 30 and placed in a large enclosure with the dispersing Campbell Blue female wolf #511. Refuge staff reported that the two were getting along well and creating excitement among four neighboring young male wolves. All the males at a nearby pen were standing on their hind legs against the fence, trying to get a look. These males could be potential mates for the recaptured females.

On May 22, Dr. Sam Luce of Alpine claimed his blue heeler dog was killed by a wolf overnight, near his home in a remote area of the Blue. Alan Armistead said that it appeared that a wolf may have killed the dog. Craig Miller promised to confer immediately with Luce about reimbursement for another cattle dog and funds to cover costs for training the replacement dog.

By early June, the elk calving in the Hawk's Nest and Campbell Blue areas was providing a plentiful food source. Four wolves from the Hawk's Nest pack, without yearling female wolf #493, traveled widely throughout their home territory. Project personnel examined the denning area of June 2, 1998, and found two dens within areas that the wolves had used for short periods of time. Scat and ungulate bones were concentrated through the den areas. No indications of pups were found. The biologists decided that probably the alpha female, #127, whelped but lost her litter before the pups were old enough to leave their den.

Paul Morey observed the Campbell Blue pair attacking an elk calf on June 3, 1998. If any births had occurred in the two nearby areas considered as den sites, there was no sign of pups.

Local residents and campers frequently observed wolves along roadsides. Project personnel had been practicing aversive conditioning toward any wolves they encountered by yelling and throwing things at the wolves. They encouraged campers and others to do the same to make the wolves stay away from humans.

In late June, the Campbell Blue pair killed an elk cow, and the female wolf #174 appeared to be limping following the kill. By July 4, she was still carrying her left leg and appeared to be extremely thin. Boyd-Heger had concerns as to whether the female would be able to survive. She and Morey brought in carcasses of an elk calf and a deer, and the Campbell Blue pair fed on them.

Since no pups had been observed in either wolf area, the forest closures around the suspected denning areas were lifted about mid-June, and supplemental feeding for the Hawk's Nest pack was stopped. During June, Boyd-Heger began writing and distributing biweekly updates on the activities of the wolves and their locations, with suggestions to the public on how to react to wolf encounters. She also spent time socializing in stores and cafes with local people, many of whom opposed wolf reintroduction. A hunter herself, Boyd-Heger swapped hunting tales with local folk, who warmed up to her friendly and straightforward approach of keeping them informed and involved with the project.

Young female wolf #493 from the Hawk's Nest pack, who had dispersed from her pack, was seen over the Fourth of July holidays in the Big Lake area, where hundreds of campers were enjoying themselves. Boyd-Heger, Morey, and Armistead spent time in the campground informing campers how to react if they encountered the wolf. A rancher who observed wolf #493 harassing a motherless calf removed the calf from the area. Later, on July 9, Armistead captured this female without injury in a modified foot-held trap in the Big Lake area. She was released in her former range and remained within this range for several weeks following return. No campers complained about her stay at the campgrounds.

At the same time, a fourteen-month-old Hawk's Nest male, #531, dispersed to a remote area in the White Mountain Apache Reservation. He later returned on his own to the Hawk's Nest range, traveling at least twenty-five miles to rejoin his pack. He remained with the pack for the remainder of the summer.

Hans Stuart, USFWS public affairs official, informed me that more than twenty pups had been born in captive-breeding facilities during the 1998 spring season, bringing the total captive Mexican wolf population up to 193, with 166 in captivity and seven in the Blue Range Area with at least twenty new pups. Mexican wolves were being cared for at forty-one facilities in the United States and Mexico, including the two preconditioning compounds at Sevilleta and Ladder Ranch.

13

The Unpredictable Wolves

Man is linked with wolf and with all of nature. To break this link is to destroy the spirit of the earth and the essence of humanity within it.

—Michael W. Fox, *The Soul of the Wolf*

Staff from channel 45, a Phoenix TV station, asked me to appear on a program with rancher Barbara Marks to discuss Mexican wolf reintroduction on July 7, 1998. Marks and I had verbally fenced previously on forums at Northern Arizona University, and because her views on wolves were diametrically opposite to mine, we provided a lively discourse. Dolores Tropiano, gossip columnist for the *Arizona Republic,* was to conduct the interview for her "Phoenix Profile." Tropiano wrote a lively column in which she shared tidbits about the rich and famous, but her background knowledge on the Mexican wolf reintroduction program was limited.

Tropiano wanted to know all about my wolf-dog and asked me what it was like to live with a wolf. She requested that I demonstrate a wolf howl and asked why it was necessary to bring the wolf back. She then interviewed Marks, who described how her husband, Billy Marks, had been threatened by five wolves while checking on a few of his cattle. She said that the wolves circled and stalked Billy until he shot his rifle into the air, and then the wolves left. Then she also told her tearful version of how Pepe, Sam Luce's blue heeler, had been killed by the Campbell Blue male wolf. Tropiano never asked her why Dr. Luce allowed the dog to run loose all night in the Campbell Blue wolves' territory.

When Tropiano asked me to comment on the dog's death, I said I was sorry about Dr. Luce's loss of his dog, but I understood he'd been well compensated by Defenders of Wildlife.

Marks laughed at my statement and claimed that Craig Miller did not respond to the dog's killing for months, even though newspapers incorrectly had reported that Defenders had compensated for the loss. Imagine my embarrassment when Marks produced a letter from Miller, apologizing for taking so long to respond to the dog's killing, and enclosing a check in the amount of $150 to compensate for the loss of the cattle dog. Fortunately, the interview was nearly over at this point.

During July, when camping at Luna Lake, I discussed the channel 45 interview with both Diane Boyd-Heger and Paul Morey. Boyd-Heger said that when she investigated the Marks's complaint the day after it occurred, the confrontation was far less dramatic. I told Boyd-Heger and Morey about my embarrassment when confronted with Miller's letter. After my bragging all over about how Defenders provides fair payments for depredation caused by wolves within two weeks, this delay in compensation didn't match Defenders's usual prompt responses, and the meager payment of $150 obviously would not cover costs for a trained cattle dog.

While I was camping in Alpine with my wolf-dog, Jato, that same July, I researched the archives administered by Peggy Gladhill, information specialist at the Alpine District Forest Service office. Gladhill made a vacant room available, where I read through valuable history of early settlement. Jato stretched out on the floor and slept.

At noon, I took a break, and Jato and I went to my camper to eat. Morey pounded on my camper door to announce great news. "A wolf pup has been sighted by volunteers with binoculars in the Campbell Blue area," he exclaimed. Apparently the female wolf #174 had given birth more than two months earlier and somehow had managed to keep her pups hidden. There was no easy way of determining whether there was a litter or this surviving pup was the only one born. This was a milestone event, because the pup was the first to be born in the wild in about fifty years and the first in the Blue since the wolves' release late in March. The pup's mother had overcome many obstacles to raise her pup to approximately twelve weeks of age. She had made her own successful transition from captivity, learned to hunt elk, and provided for herself and the pup with the help of only her mate, male wolf #166.

On July 17, an area closure went into effect within a one-mile radius of the rendezvous sight where the pup had been observed. Biologists reported that the Campbell Blue female appeared to have gained weight following her injury and was getting around quite well. The biologists continued their frequent monitoring on the ground and in the air, sometimes two or three times daily. They did not know the sex of the pup because they avoided getting too close to the wolves so as not to disturb them. A few days following the sighting of the pup, Boyd-Heger said she heard an elk bugling in the throes of death and later discovered the Campbell Blue pair and their pup gorging on the kill.

The Campbell Blue pair explored the country with their pup. Biologists expressed concern that there might be interactions between them and the Hawk's Nest pack. Boyd-Heger told me that the two packs had finally discovered each other and were seen having a confrontation in the middle of State Route 191. Naturally, biologists feared that the Hawk's Nest wolves would kill the pup. Later on, the young Hawk's Nest female #493, who had previously dispersed to Big Lake, was seen with blood on her ear and hip. Boyd-Heger suspected an altercation between the two packs.

During my July visit to Alpine, Boyd-Heger visited me at my Luna Lake campsite. During our conversation, I sensed her concern over difficulties in implementing more effective preconditioning protocol. She wanted to see more vegetative screening provided at the Sevilleta facility and far less human contact. She wanted the caretakers to stop feeding the wolves only dry kibbled canine food and use road-killed meat. She believed that the locations of two of the acclimation pens chosen for the initial release were too close to Alpine.

Boyd-Heger invited me to go on one of her nightly tracking sessions and suggested that we take Jato to the Mexican wolf office, where Morey could take care of him while we tried to locate female wolf #493. I jumped into the front of the truck, and she hoisted 130-pound Jato up on top of me, where I tried to contain him sprawled across my lap and attempted to keep him from interfering with Boyd-Heger's driving. He squirmed and pawed during the three-mile drive. We left Jato in Morey's care and Boyd-Heger and I drove off to track the wolf.

We made about ten stops, during which #493 kept moving through the rugged forested hills and canyons. I was impressed with Boyd-Heger's ability to orient compass readings to the location indicated by the telemetry signals. Dusk was descending rapidly, and although we never sighted female wolf #493, the telemetry signals indicated that she was as close as three hundred yards away from us at one point. I told Boyd-Heger, "I'm getting goose bumps hearing that beep-beep-beep and knowing it's really #493, roaming the Blue."

Later Boyd-Heger told me that both the Campbell Blue and Hawk's Nest wolves had made several successful elk kills during July and August. Because the Campbell Blue wolves did not show any indication of returning to their former range, closure was lifted and signs removed. This pair killed a cow elk on August 2, about four hundred yards from a corral full of cattle. A rancher observed the pair with their pup but said that the wolves did not bother his cattle. He moved them from the corral to a grazing area without incident, while the wolves remained on their elk kill.

Upon returning to Phoenix after my July camp-out in Alpine, I called Terry Johnson to discuss my concerns over Boyd-Heger's growing frustrations in gaining cooperation from the Albuquerque USFWS staff to implement preconditioning changes that she believed would improve released wolves' behavior. Johnson admitted that he had similar concerns and wished that the Albuquerque staff would recognize the value of Boyd-Heger's recommendations.

On Friday, August 7, 1998, the opening day of bear-hunting season, a private citizen reported to the wolf biologists that he saw a wolf lying near a forest road, and within minutes the biologists received the mortality signal from female wolf #174's collar. They found the dead female lying just five yards from an elk calf carcass. Following preliminary examination, wildlife specialist Alan Armistead said that he believed she had been killed by a mountain lion. Barry Burkhart of the *Arizona Republic* reported that John Phelps, furbearer specialist for the AGFD, had a different opinion after he looked at the dead wolf: "A chunk of its side was ripped out which could have been consistent with being shot with a high-powered rifle." Wolf #174's body was shipped to the USFWS forensic lab in Oregon to determine the cause of death. The female wolf's death was a definite loss to the program, but because the pup was old enough to be weaned, biologists hoped that the pup would be able to survive with just the father, wolf #166. Ground-based and aircraft radio telemetry continued daily. The Campbell Blue pup was observed traveling with its father and appeared to be getting larger and fatter. Boyd-Heger estimated the pup's weight at about twenty pounds.

The Hawk's Nest five wolves remained together and expanded their range to include much of the former Campbell

Blue pack's home range. About the same time, Boyd-Heger examined an elk kill made by the Hawk's Nest pack that proved to be a six-year-old elk in prime age but suffering from a broken femur. This was an old injury sustained prior to the wolf attack.

From August 15 to August 23, the Campbell Blue alpha male, #166, was observed in Williams Valley caring for the pup. Following his mate's death, the male temporarily lost the use of his left front leg, and biologists suspected that the injury may have happened during a fight with another predator over killed prey meat. The biologists provided an elk hindquarter because they thought male wolf #166 might have difficulty taking live prey with the injury. Boyd-Heger last saw the Campbell Blue pup on August 18 with its father. A local resident reported sighting them together on August 22, four miles southwest of Alpine. The male was still favoring his left front foot. The pup was then more than three months old and appeared fat and healthy.

After August 22, the pup vanished. It was never again observed with the male #166, who, on August 24, was observed by project personnel near Nutrioso. At this point, they assumed that the pup must be dead, because the Campbell Blue male, who had previously been so dedicated to tending to the pup's needs, now was alone.

The same adventurous female Hawk's Nest wolf #493 that had previously dispersed to Big Lake had again left her pack after August 20 and was located near the Hawk's Nest range. After leaving her pack, she was observed several times by project personnel and local residents along State Route 191, south of Alpine.

The remaining four Hawk's Nest wolves remained together, but the alpha female, #127, dropped her collar on August 10. Apparently her head got stuck inside a hollow log as she pursued small prey, and she escaped after slipping her collar. A tremendous amount of excavation around the site and torn-up soil along the log indicated that other pack members may have attempted to free her. The biologists found the radio collar near the log, but there was no evidence of blood or injury. The Hawk's Nest wolves minus female #493 were observed together by a bear hunter after the female lost her collar. Boyd-Heger reported that project personnel made intensive attempts to re-capture the female by using free-range darting with a drug-loaded transmitter dart in order to install a new radio collar on her. After several days without success, they abandoned this effort. August 29 telemetry monitoring indicated the four wolves of this pack were traveling together.

During August 1998, the tribal council for the White Mountain Apache Tribe passed a resolution endorsing limited re-establishment of Mexican wolves on their reservation. Wolf recovery would occur by dispersal of wolves reintroduced to the Apache National Forest and natural reproduction by these dispersions on the reservation. These wolves would be man-aged according to an agreement to be later reached between the tribe and the USFWS.

Dispersal patterns of the Campbell Blue male #166 and the Hawk's Nest female #493 led biologists to believe that perhaps they might get together. The two wolves had been located in the same areas but at different times. The biologists believed they must have been aware of each other's presence, because of scent marks, scats, and tracks, but apparently there was no attraction between them or any indication that they had ren-dezvoused. Project personnel continued their intensive moni-toring of the two dispersers with telemetry, and both wolves appeared to be in good condition. Supplemental feeding was suspended for all wolves.

On October 8, 1998, I met Will and Jan Holder at the Phoenix Farmers Market, held at Heritage Square, where they were sell-ing their Ervin's Natural Beef. Their product was getting lots of attention and attracting new markets. The Holders told me they had recently entered into a marketing agreement with Tucson's Cooperative Warehouse, which maintains outlets in eight other states. Several other Arizona ranchers were interested in forming a cooperative with the Holders that would require adhering to their criteria for beef production.

Later that fall, Defenders announced that they would endorse beef produced by ranchers who agreed not to kill predators. Ranchers would apply a label to the product, signifying Defenders's seal of approval. With their growing market for Ervin's Natural Beef, the Holders were reluctant to join Defenders's Wolf Country Beef program because they did not want to replace their Ervin's Natural Beef label with Defenders's Wolf Country Beef label. Finally Defenders agreed to allow the Holders to retain their own label and just add Defenders's endorsement label, and the Holders consented to sign on to the Wolf Country Beef program.

During September and October, Mexican wolf project personnel continued close surveillance of all remaining wolves in the Blue Range Area. Late in September, the Campbell Blue male #166 was located in the Campbell Blue Creek area near his former rendezvous site, but no further evidence of the Campbell Blue pup was encountered.

Sometimes the Hawk's Nest pack remained together during September, and sometimes they traveled as loners, but they were located every day and seen on many occasions by various project personnel. On the morning of September 14, the Hawk's Nest pack killed an elk calf in the Josh Ranch pasture. Boyd-Heger; Nick Smith, of the New Mexico Department of Game and Fish; and Laura Lagos, a volunteer from Spain, discovered the dead elk calf in the pasture with cattle, horses, and a burro present. The ranch caretaker and project personnel observed the wolves in the pasture and saw no aggressive behavior toward the livestock. To be on the safe side, project personnel dragged the elk calf's carcass outside the pasture and onto nearby Forest Service public land. The wolves left the ranch the next day after finishing their meal. On September 17, the Hawk's Nest pack killed an adult cow elk near Beaver Creek.

On September 24, Ed Heger found the Hawk's Nest wolves near a dead domestic calf. The rancher who owned the cattle joined Boyd-Heger, Smith, and Jaybrad Miller of Wildlife Services, formerly ADC, at the allotment, and they examined the calf carcass and discussed what had occurred. Miller necropsied the calf, which appeared to have been dead less than forty-eight hours. With further investigation, he determined that it had been killed by a mountain lion, moved three times, and partially buried each time. Project personnel removed the dead domestic calf to prevent the wolves from feeding upon it and getting a taste for beef.

Boyd-Heger reported, "We captured young Hawk's Nest male #532 for a routine examination, and he appeared in excellent health, weighing seventy pounds." She said that local residents saw the uncollared alpha female #127 several times up until September 19, but after that date she suddenly vanished. Previously, she had not displayed dispersing tendencies, and her sudden disappearance was surprising. Boyd-Heger suspected that she may have been killed.

As time went on, I speculated that the fate of this wolf and the missing pup might well have been cases of "shoot, shovel, and shut up." Without collars, both the pup and female #127 could have been shot and disposed of without any mortality signal.

14

When Will the Killings Stop?

The Moving Finger writes; and, having writ,
Moves on; nor all thy Piety nor Wit
Shall lure it back to cancel half a Line,
Nor all thy Tears wash out a Word of it.
—*The Rubaiyat of Omar Khayyam*

Two newspaper reporters called me on Monday, October 19, 1998, to get my reaction to the death of female #493. Her death came as a complete shock, and I was heartbroken, because this wolf was the last remaining female in the Blue Range Area. Paul Morey had told me just two days before she was killed that he'd seen her, and she had appeared in excellent condition. Public affairs staff members in Albuquerque were apparently under a gag rule and would only state that the body of #493 was found and had been shipped to the forensic lab in Ashland, Oregon, for necropsy.

On October 21, Diane Boyd-Heger called to tell me she was under orders not to give out any information concerning the wolf's death. She did say that Paul Morey and Nick Smith had been out monitoring on that Sunday and had detected the mortality signal coming from #493. They had gone immediately to the site of her death and found her body. Boyd-Heger said that the USFWS investigative team was investigating the incident.

I knew that the necropsy could take weeks, and I also knew that if the wolf's death had been caused by death from natural causes, the USFWS probably would not initiate activity by the investigative team. I suspected that the wolf had been shot.

On Thursday, November 6, the USFWS issued a press release revealing that the Campbell Blue alpha female, #174, erroneously reported as killed by a mountain lion, was actually killed by a high-powered rifle. This confirmed AGFD's John Phelps's earlier deduction. The necropsy of the Campbell Blue alpha female, #174, also indicated that she had five placenta scars, indicating that she had given birth to five pups, only one of which was ever seen by project personnel before it vanished.

Hearing this, I remembered that this was the wolf that Interior Secretary Bruce Babbitt carried into the pen on January 26. I wondered how he'd react when he learned "his wolf" had been shot. With the Service's admission that #174 had been shot, the series of shootings was beginning to shape up more and more as an organized plan to destroy the Mexican wolf recovery program.

The USFWS had received the necropsy report on female wolf #174 in September but withheld the information from the public for two months. USFWS public affairs staff claimed the reason for the lengthy delay was that the law enforcement team were hoping the suspect would reveal himself through conversations that would ultimately get back to them. Public outrage over the Albuquerque staff's continued secrecy on the status of the Mexican wolves mounted.

On November 10, the USFWS issued a press release announcing the death of yet another Hawk's Nest wolf, male #532, near the Arizona–New Mexico border. For the first time, Babbitt publicly voiced his dismay over the series of wolf shootings in a press release issued by the USFWS: "All of these losses are tragic because the wolves were displaying all of the right behaviors in the wild. Each of them were successfully hunting elk and avoiding livestock."

The mounting death toll of the Mexican wolves jolted the USFWS into action. They offered a $10,000 reward, authorized under the ESA, for information leading to the conviction of the person or persons responsible for the Mexican wolf deaths. The deliberate killing of these wolves was a criminal violation of both federal and state laws. It carried a federal penalty of up to $100,000 and up to one year in prison, in addition to state and criminal penalties.

In a CNN television segment, Babbitt stated that he believed the wolf killings resulted from a systematic attempt to destroy the Mexican wolf reintroduction program. Babbitt's public expression of concern prompted Nancy Kaufman, regional director, to make a statement published in a USFWS press release: "Although we must await confirmation on the cause of death from our National Forensics Lab, we're viewing this apparent shooting as an attempt to sabotage wolf recovery. We're going to hit this investigation hard. Our law enforcement team in the field includes agents from the U.S. Fish and Wildlife Service, the Arizona Game and Fish Department, and the New Mexico Department of Game and Fish. To prevent any further losses, we will need the public's support and help."

On November 11, Steve Yozwiak, reporter for the *Arizona Republic,* quoted rancher Barbara Marks as saying, "I don't know that I can go as far as to say that I condemn that [shooting]. I don't condone it, but I don't condemn it." Boyd-Heger told me that Dink Robarts, who had protested the wolf reintroduction, totally surprised her with a genuine display of shock and anger over the continued wolf killing. He advised her to get a new female for lone male wolf #166 and put them in a pen together to mate.

It appeared that the USFWS law enforcement to date had been totally ineffective. Their mishandling of Richard Humphrey's case, in letting him off scot-free, enraged not only wolf supporters but also much of the general public. The regional USFWS flawed decision on this case had literally blown up in their faces. As predicted, this decision openly invited other perpetrators to shoot wolves without penalty.

In her November 13 article in the *Tucson Citizen,* Carla McClain reported that Defenders of Wildlife had matched the $10,000 reward. She quoted Rodger Schlickeisen, president of Defenders, as saying, "It's a real shame that some people are so selfish that they are unwilling to coexist with nature instead of destroying it. Defenders will do everything we can to help bring those who are committing these crimes to justice. These killings will not go unpunished."

McClain further reported that Michael Blake, author of *Dances with Wolves,* donated $5,000, and the Southwest Center for Biodiversity added another $5,000, as had a coalition of New Mexico environmental groups. The Grand Canyon chapter of the Sierra Club contributed $5,000 to the wolf-killer reward fund, and Michael Blake later doubled his donation to $10,000. Defenders added another $5,000 to bring the amount to $50,000.

On November 12 through 14, 1998, Defenders of Wildlife conducted a wolf conference in Seattle, Washington. About 450 wolf advocates gathered to learn more about wolf restoration throughout the United States and Mexico, and I participated in a Mexican wolf forum. Highlights of the conference included talks by Estella Leopold, daughter of Aldo Leopold; 'Asta Bowen, author of *Hungry for Home*; Doug Smith, National Park Service project leader for the Yellowstone wolf; Ed Bangs, USFWS gray wolf recovery leader for the northwest Rocky Mountain region; and Diane Boyd-Heger.

I was pleasantly surprised by being made a guest of honor at the Friday night banquet, at which I was seated at the head table near Rodger Schlickeisen. Following the program, Schlickeisen presented me with Defenders's Conservation Award of Excellence. Somehow I managed to keep my emotions in check as I thanked him. I was amazed at being singled out for such an honor and felt pretty humble in the presence of so many wolf experts. After accepting the award, I presented Schlickeisen with P.A.WS.'s check for $2,000 for Defenders's wolf compensation fund. Before disbanding in May 1998, P.A.WS. members had decided to split their remaining funds between Defenders of Wildlife and the AGFD Mexican Wolf Trust Fund. The AGFD donation was made later on.

Boyd-Heger generously commended me on my award and told me that she would be returning to Alpine after her Saturday presentation. Once back in Alpine, she had to jump in her truck and drive to the Ladder Ranch to pick up the two females that were to be introduced to the Campbell Blue alpha male wolf, #166, and the Hawk's Nest alpha male, #131. One of the females, #486, born at the Rio Grande Zoo, would be transferred to the Campbell Blue acclimation pen to be joined later by recaptured male wolf #131. I was happy to learn that the other female, #482, one of Rosa's pups born at the Phoenix Zoo, would be taken to the Engineer Spring pen to be joined by recaptured male #166.

On November 17, 1998, with the air crisp and the skies blue and sunny in the highlands of the Blue, Secretary Bruce Babbitt and USFWS and AGFD officials carried female wolf #486 to the Campbell Blue acclimation pen. I was flying home from Seattle on the Monday when all of this took place but later picked up details in an article published that same day by Steve Yozwiak in the *Arizona Republic*.

"The wolf is here to stay," Babbitt firmly stated and made it clear that he would assist the law enforcement officers in bringing the wolf killers to justice. "It's just incomprehensible that people would view this (wolf) as a threat, and that they would resort to this kind of violence. The future of these rare and beautiful creatures must not be jeopardized by bullets and senseless killings. We want to work with local communities and solve these crimes. We are committed to the recovery of the

Mexican wolf and the goals of the Endangered Species Act." Peter Umhofer, special assistant to Jamie Clark, director of USFWS, added that bringing the wolf killers to justice was the Interior's top priority.

Not long after the arrival of the new females, the only surviving wolf in the wild, yearling male #531, who had a history of dispersing, was gunned down near Hawley Lake, about thirteen miles from McNary, on the White Mountain Apache Reservation. Secretary Babbitt was quick to express his abhorrence to the latest killing but vowed that the wolf reintroduction program would continue until the goal of at least one hundred wolves in the area for three years had been reached.

Ranchers were calling for abandoning the experiment. On Wednesday, November 25, Steve Yozwiak of the *Arizona Republic* quoted Barbara Marks as saying, "How much money do they have to spend before they admit that it's a failure for the wolves and for the community?" The same article reported that Kieran Suckling, president of the Southwest Center for Biodiversity, stated that cattle ranching should be phased out throughout the area, and unneeded roads in the national forests should be closed. He called for complete wilderness status for the entire area, which would ban mechanized vehicles.

Rumors abounded that a wealthy Catron County rancher was posting a bounty of $10,000 for any dead Mexican wolf. As reported in the November 15 *Arizona Daily Star,* rancher Rose Coleman-Autrey told reporter Rhonda Bodfield that she was happy to hear the wolves were being shot, because she would like nothing more than to see the program terminated. She predicted that the shootings would not stop. "We started with eleven and we're down to three. There's enough people who don't want the program who will see to it that it doesn't materialize."

Such inflammatory rhetoric from both sides of the issue could do nothing but rekindle old antirancher sentiment among the environmental community and further polarize the two communities to the point of verbal range wars. As I had learned during my eleven years' work as an advocate for the Mexican wolf, polarization had never resolved a single issue.

The full impact of the five wolf deaths really hit me over the Thanksgiving holidays. I had mental flashbacks of the gleam in the eyes of Campbell Blue alpha female #174, when she first leaped to freedom back on January 26, 1998. She had later given birth to five pups, and although only one survived, she had successfully made the transition from captivity to the open forest. But her freedom was short-lived when she was abruptly shot dead. I could imagine the thunderous shot that had taken out her whole shoulder when she was blown away by a high-powered rifle. Equally egregious to me were the series of wolf killings that followed. This systematic picking off of nearly every free wolf was beyond my comprehension.

As I had done on so many occasions when I was really downhearted about the Mexican wolf program, I called Terry Johnson of AGFD for a good heart-to-heart talk. While Johnson was not able to give me any good news, he had strong praise for the progress Boyd-Heger had made in securing coopera-tion from the local people. He said he had a lot of faith in the Department's Operation Game Thief, and mentioned pre-vious cases of excessive lion and bear killings where they had successfully tracked down the violators and brought them to justice.

After the Thanksgiving break, I had a good conversation with Boyd-Heger. She reported that the Hawk's Nest male #131 and his new mate #486 had been viewed with binoculars snug-gling together in the Campbell Blue pen. The Campbell Blue male #166 and his new mate #482 appeared to be bonding well in the Engineer Spring pen, but project personnel were keeping their distance to eliminate human exposure.

Boyd-Heger told me that during the recapture procedure, both males were shot with tranquilizing darts. "Male wolf #131 developed hypothermia when his internal heating system didn't regulate properly after he was tranquilized. We brought him to the wolf office in his crate to protect him from overnight freezing temperatures while the effects of the drug wore off. An Alpine rancher provided alfalfa hay for us to place around his body to keep him warm." Boyd-Heger declined to identify the rancher who wanted to help the biologists in their endeavors even though he didn't particularly like wolves. She added, "By morning, male #131 was reinvigorated and ready to meet his new mate."

Horror stories about the wolf killings were given national media coverage by CNN, NBC's *Today Show,* and *NBC Nightly News.* A reporter for the *NBC Nightly News,* who was preparing a five-minute segment about the Mexican wolf killings, called to add my perspective. He requested that I make the nearly six hundred-mile round trip to Alpine at my own expense so that he could film a few sentences from Barbara Marks and me having an argument about wolves over breakfast at the Bear Wallow Cafe. I suggested to him that their Phoenix affiliate could cover my statements for his segment and save me the long drive, but the reporter was only interested in filming a face-to-face conflict in Alpine. I declined.

I was surprised when Mike Lucckino, special agent of the USFWS investigative team, called to query me on what I might know about the wolf killings. I told him I had absolutely no evidence of any kind that would point to a wolf killer, only a gut reaction that the wolf killings had been systematically planned to sabotage the Mexican wolf reintroduction process. I could not accept the killings as random shootings by hunters who thought they were killing coyotes. I mentioned Barbara Marks's disparaging remarks to the press but admitted I didn't believe she or her husband were wolf killers. I was shocked when Lucckino asked me who Barbara Marks was. I thought at first he was joking, as anyone spending time in the Alpine area investigating for even a short period of time should have been well aware of Barbara Marks.

Barbara Marks issued a press release on December 1, through the Arizona Beef Council of the Arizona Cattlemen's Association (formerly Arizona Cattle Growers Association, or ACGA), containing inflammatory statements. The press release stated that "the wolves have been drugged, trapped, caged, and relocated on a regular basis but even worse, they have not adapted to living in the wild and are virtually starving." Marks alleged a high level of wolf-human interaction. "If you had a dog in the same condition as these wolves, the Humane Society would prosecute you for mistreatment and neglect." She called the "cruel experiment" a travesty. She went on to say, "There have been accusations that the wolves are being shot by 'eco-terrorists,' with the implication that ranchers are responsible for trying to wipe out this experimental group of wolves" (pp. 1–2).

The USFWS quickly issued a press release that included a "talking points" fact sheet. Although they admitted that three of the wolves had temporarily appeared thin, none were starving. The USFWS refuted Marks's inaccurate claims and said that the level of wolf-human interaction alleged had not been reported to the USFWS or the AGFD. The fact sheet concluded with, "A continuing problem facing the wolf reintroduction effort is misinformation being distributed by a variety of groups, both favoring and opposing the program. The only apparent impediment to wolf recovery is that too many wolves are being shot by humans" (pp. 1–2).

Adding further fury to local residents' opposition to the wolf project, the USFWS investigative team mailed out an eight-page questionnaire to local New Mexico hunters, aimed at uncovering evidence of the wolf killings. The harsh tone of the language created anger among the hunting community. As reported in the March 1999 *American Hunter,* the questionnaire began: "We have reached the determination that a Mexican Gray wolf was found dead from a gunshot wound near Unit 15A (Luna, NM) during the time you were hunting, November 1998. How would you explain this?"

Recipients were further grilled with such questions as, "Do you know who shot the wolf? Did you shoot the wolf? Did you take part in shooting the wolf?" The recipients' wrath was further incited when the inquisition concluded with these questions: "Should we believe your answers to the questions? If your answer to the last question was yes, give us one reason why. What would you say if it was later determined that the answers on this form are not the truth?"

Why the USFWS investigative team wasted their time and taxpayer money preparing and mailing out such an offensive questionnaire when they should have been out in the field investigating tips and encouraging cooperation from the local residents and hunters, I will never know. When I discussed the questionnaire with Johnson, he said, "It ranks as the stupidest government action I've seen in twenty years!"

As reported by an Associated Press article in the *Arizona Republic* on December 20, 1998, members of the New Mexico congressional delegation, Representative Joe Skeen (R) and Senators Pete Domeneci (R) and Jeff Bingamon (D), were quick to publicly express outrage over the questionnaire. Upon learning about the questionnaire, USFWS Director Jamie Clark demanded that it be withdrawn and ordered that a letter of apology be sent to every recipient. Senator Bingamon said that although the wolf shootings were tragic, "this questionnaire inverts the very principle of our legal system."

In December 1998, I heard a rumor that Diane Boyd-Heger was leaving the Mexican wolf program. Confirmation of this rumor in a conversation with Boyd-Heger really sent me into a tailspin. It was my belief Boyd-Heger's professional stature and her extensive experience with wolves would not allow her to further tolerate the USFWS Albuquerque staff's denials to implement, what she believed, were needed changes for more effective protocol on the preconditioning of the wolves and on releasing them in more remote locations.

She had been offered a permanent position in Montana with Ed Bangs, USFWS coordinator for the northwest Rocky Mountain wolf program. With her love of Montana, no one could blame her for not turning down such an opportunity. However, I did not believe for a moment that she would leave the Mexican wolf program just for a return to Montana. With her experience, Boyd-Heger could have accepted a higher-paying position in Montana or elsewhere the year before. When she had accepted the Mexican wolf position early in 1998, she had stated her intent to stay with the program until the reintroduction goals had been accomplished.

When I expressed my conclusions to Boyd-Heger as to why she decided to leave the Mexican wolf program, she answered with a very professional "No comment." She told me she had truly enjoyed working with the staff of AGFD and that she had learned to love the community of Alpine. She believed she had made major inroads into securing the cooperation of many of the local people in assisting her in the wolf program. She assured me that she would be actively recruiting her replacement and would participate in the candidate selection.

Following my discussion with Boyd-Heger, I spoke briefly on the phone with Johnson, who agreed with my assessment of why she resigned the Mexican wolf position. He said she had displayed the same professional attitude to him when she resigned the position and would not comment concerning any difficulties she had had with the Albuquerque staff. However, he was well aware of the strained relationships that must have made it difficult for her to continue her responsibilities. Johnson assured me that AGFD would make every effort to hire an experienced wolf biologist by January 15, 1999—Boyd-Heger's exit date. We agreed that it would be impossible to find anyone with her outstanding talents.

The two pairs of Mexican wolves awaited release to the wild near the middle of December. The Hawk's Nest male wolf #131 and his mate, #486, were living in the Campbell Blue pen, and Campbell Blue male wolf #166 and his mate, #482, in the Engineer Spring pen. The wolf biologists prepared the wolves for release by spraying them with bright orange, yellow, and pink splotches to clearly set them apart from any other wildlife. No longer could any shooter claim that he thought the animals were coyotes. No fanfare accompanied the release of the two pairs, as the wolf biologists opened the far sides of the acclimation pens, allowing the wolves to escape to freedom.

Following release, both pairs traveled together for three or four days. The Campbell Blue pair, male #166 and female #482, remained together and explored the surrounding area. The Hawk's Nest female #486 left male #131 after just a few days and struck out on her own.

Male #131 went alone over to Luna, New Mexico. On January 9, 1999, project personnel found a dead dog near wolf #131's location, but when Alan Armistead examined the dog's body, he discovered that the dog had died from a gunshot wound and had not been injured or fed upon by a wolf. Two dead cows were found in the area, but the wolf had not fed on either cow. Project personnel talked to the rancher who owned them, and he buried their remains. Wolf #131 returned to Arizona.

A rancher in the Blue area threw out domestic pig entrails left over from butchering, and male wolf #131 fed on them. Project personnel visited the ranch and talked to the rancher before they removed all remaining carrion. They then drove male wolf #131 out of the area using aversive conditioning.

At dusk on December 23, 1998, the Campbell Blue male wolf #166 and female wolf #482 visited a hunters' camp four miles from the acclimation pen. The hunters should have driven the wolves away immediately by shooting their guns in the air, but they told the visiting project personnel they enjoyed watching the wolves investigate their camp. The wolves found a white-tailed deer carcass the hunters had hung from a tree after killing it, and consumed about twenty pounds. Project personnel examined the carcass and the wolf signs. After discussing the situation with the hunters, they decided to remain at the camp, hoping that the wolves would return. The next day, the wolves returned to the camp, and the project staff aversely conditioned them with rubber slugs and chased them away while yelling and throwing rocks. The wolves ran off and did not return before the hunters' departure on December 26. Supplemental feeding was discontinued.

My Christmas holidays with my daughters, Bonnie and Bettie, seemed overshadowed by the series of tragic Mexican wolf killings that had occurred during their first year of freedom, plus the imminent loss of Diane Boyd-Heger from the project. Soon after the holiday period, I contacted Terry Johnson and Bill Van Pelt about the possibility of attending one of the placements of additional wolves in the Blue area, scheduled for January 8 and 13, 1999. Van Pelt suggested I make arrangements to accompany video specialist and producer Gary Shafer and photographer George Andrejko for the January 8 placement of five wolves in the Engineer Spring acclimation pen.

On January 8, 1999, the skies were shrouded in dark clouds above the Apache Forest, unlike the bright, sunny day that had greeted the first wolf pack a year before. Perhaps this ominous beginning bode well for a sunny future for the wolves.

The two trucks driven by Diane Boyd-Heger and Dave Parsons, accompanied by Colleen Buchanan, bearing the five Mexican wolves from Ladder Ranch arrived at about four o'clock in the afternoon. Boyd-Heger greeted me with a big hug and invited me to stand in the entry area of the pen while the wolves were carried in. She directed the unloading and placement of the crates inside the pen. As Morey opened the first crate, the alpha male, #183, burst from the metal cage and bounded to the far side of the pen. He was a large Mexican wolf, probably weighing ninety pounds, and his frisky movements, upon being released from his crate, displayed his joy at being allowed to stretch his long legs and run. His mate, #168, was not quite as anxious to leave her confinement, but after coaxing from Boyd-Heger, #168 ran out to join her mate.

The three eight-month-old pups, one female, #554, and two males, #555 and #556, were very reluctant to leave their crates. One male ran out when the rear of his crate was tipped. For the other two, Boyd-Heger advised unscrewing the top half of the crate to allow the pups to see the other wolves, and when they did, they ran to join them. Once all five were running free within the pen, they explored the perimeters of their holding area. These wolves were named the Strayhorse pack, after a nearby creek.

On January 13, 1999, four more wolves transported from the Sevilleta facility were placed in the Turkey Creek pen. These wolves, named the Pipestem pack, consisted of alpha male #208, his mate, #191, and their two female eight-month-old offspring, #562 and #563. Project personnel living in a tent about a half mile away from the acclimation pen monitored their activities daily using binoculars.

On January 15, Boyd-Heger's last day in the project office, she called to say goodbye before she left for Montana the next day. She told me about a meeting she had just attended in Albuquerque, where consultant members of the Mexican wolf program met with staff from both AGFD and the USFWS. The consultants, Mike Phillips, David Mech, Steve Fritts, and Ed Bangs, all believed that we must not count the Mexican wolf program as a failure because of the tragic losses in 1998. Bangs discussed difficulties the Yellowstone wolves had faced when attempting to set up territories outside of the park boundaries. Phillips said that the red wolf program had lost seventy-six wolves before they had established successful packs in the Alligator River National Wildlife Refuge. Mech praised the biological success the released Mexican wolves had exhibited in adjusting to the wild, killing their own food, and producing pups.

Boyd-Heger hoped for the success of the Mexican wolf program and repeated her profound respect for the staff of AGFD. After she left the Mexican wolf program for Montana, I learned indirectly that major changes were planned for the Mexican wolf program by the Albuquerque USFWS offices. There had been heavy public criticism of the poor 1998 site selections, which may have contributed to the tragic wolf killings. Now the implication existed that Diane Boyd-Heger may have resigned because of a lack of Albuquerque USFWS staff cooperation. Following her departure, several of Boyd-Heger's suggestions, including less human contact and more remote releases, were finally implemented.

Renewed Hope for the Mexican Wolves

We all strive for safety, prosperity, comfort, long life, and dullness. The deer strives with his supple legs, the cowman with trap and poison, the statesman with pen, the most of us with machines, votes, and dollars, but it all comes to the same thing: peace in our time. A measure of success in this is all well enough, and perhaps a requisite to objective thinking, but too such safety seems to yield only danger in the long run. Perhaps this is behind Thoreau's dictum: In wildness is the salvation of the world. Perhaps this is the hidden meaning in the howl of the wolf, long known among mountains, but seldom perceived among men.

—Aldo Leopold, *A Sand County Almanac*

At the January 22, 1999, AGF Commission meeting, on behalf of P.A.WS., I presented a check for $2,000 to Terry Johnson for the Mexican Wolf Trust Fund to support the projects of the Alpine Mexican wolf program. Richard Remington, supervisor of the Department's Pinetop office, presented a Mexican wolf program status report. Then he announced, "Following consideration of several candidates for the Mexican wolf biologist position, the unanimous choice of the selection committee that included Bill Van Pelt, Dan Groebner, and Diane Boyd-Heger, was Val Asher."

In 1985, Asher had worked on an Earth Watch research project in Ely, Minnesota, and in 1989, she worked a year on David Mech's wolf project, also in Ely. She earned her bachelor's degree in environmental studies, with a concentration in wildlife management and animal behavior, in 1992 from Warren Wilson College in Swannanoa, North Carolina. The same year she accepted a position with Yellowstone National Park, trapping small mammals and collaring coyotes for Bob Crabtree.

In the winter of 1992, she worked on a wolf-ungulate research project in Glacier National Park. In May 1993, she accepted a position as caretaker and handler for a captive pack of wolves in Stanley, Idaho, owned by a private filmmaker and photographer. In May 1994, she was hired as a biologist for the USFWS in Boise, Idaho, to work on a wolf reintroduction project. In the winters of 1995 and 1996, she was sent to Canada to assist with the translocation of wolves from Canada to Yellowstone and central Idaho. Much of her duties for the next three years had focused on tracking the wolves in Idaho and interacting with landowners on wolf conflicts.

Several weeks after the placement of the Strayhorse pack of five wolves into the Engineer Spring pen, project biologists observed severe fence-fighting between this pack and the Campbell Blue pair, male #166 and female #482, who were frequenting the perimeter of the Engineer Spring pen. Attempts to discourage this behavior with electric fencing around the pen and other aversive techniques did not stop the fights. Biologists decided to temporarily return the Strayhorse five to Ladder Ranch, to allow the Campbell Blue pair to settle down and select a breeding location.

When a veterinarian examined the Strayhorse wolves, he found two of them had minor injuries. Male wolf #556 had lost a toe and had infected cuts on one paw. He was taken to an isolation facility at Sevilleta for further treatment. The female #554 had a torn ear and a swollen toe. She and the remaining wolves in the pack were treated with antibiotics and held at Ladder Ranch.

On Tuesday morning, March 15, the biologists opened the gate on the Turkey Creek pen and released the Pipestem pack, including the alpha male, #208, and his mate, #191, with their two female offspring, #562 and #563, now ten months old. Before the release, the biologists decided that for this and all future releases, the wolves' collars would be wound with fluorescent tape to indicate that they were wolves, not coyotes. Female wolf #562 traveled more widely than the rest of her pack, and on several monitoring forays, project personnel were not able to find her.

The following Friday, three of the former Strayhorse pack, the alpha male, #183, the alpha female, #168, and one male pup, #555, were brought back from temporary residence at Ladder Ranch. The injured female wolf #554 remained at Ladder Ranch to recover from her wounds. Surgery was performed on the pack's other male, #556, to correct injuries sustained during the fence-fighting episode. He recovered from the wounds and was placed in captivity with his sibling, female #554. Because of the injuries these wolves had suffered, the biologists decided to return them permanently to a captive-breeding facility.

The Strayhorse pack was renamed the Gavilan pack to avoid confusion between area names and was placed into a semi-soft release pen, or mesh pen, in a remote area near the New Mexico border and Coalson Peak. The mesh pen was constructed of heavy-gauge nylon mesh reinforced with live electric fencing, and it enhanced the biologists' ability to acclimate wolves in remote wilderness locations where transporting steel-link fencing would be nearly impossible. The fencing was intended to retain the reintroduced wolves for a few days while they became accustomed to the area.

On Sunday, March 20, a motorist on State Route 191 saw one young Pipestem female wolf, #563, lying dead along the side of the road. The wolf's body was shipped to the USFWS forensic lab in Oregon for necropsy to establish cause of death. Results of the necropsy determined that a vehicle had struck the youngster.

On Thursday, April 1, 1999, rancher Scott Dieringer reported to Alan Armistead that he had witnessed two of the Pipestem pack wolves harassing his dog. He reported that he fired his gun in the air several times and then threw rocks at them to make them run away. On Tuesday, April 6, the wolves returned and fought with his dog. He found one of his calves dead and called Armistead to determine cause of death. Toni Williams, staff writer for *The Copper Era,* published in Clifton, Arizona, reported on April 14 that the wolves apparently had been attracted to the area by a dead bull and cow that had died of natural causes. No effort had been made to remove the carcasses.

After examining the dead calf, Armistead stated that he could not determine whether the death was caused by wolves, bears, or eagles that had been seen circling the area. Because of the inconclusive reports, Defenders reimbursed the rancher for 50 percent of the market value of the calf, about $250.

The second week in April, Frosty Taylor of AGFD told me that the transfer of the Sevilleta pair, female #189 and male #190, by mule back to a remote acclimation pen, which had been scheduled for April 1, had been postponed when thirty inches of snow fell on the forest. Soon after, Sevilleta manager Colleen Buchanan announced that female #189 had given birth to four pups. Transfer from Sevilleta to the nylon-mesh pen was rescheduled for early summer, when the pups would better adjust to the transition to the wild.

Buchanan also reported that Campbell Blue female wolf #511, who had first shared a pen with the Hawk's Nest female wolf #494, had been put into a pen on September 14, 1998, with three sibling males and allowed to select a mate. Among the three males, #509 was the largest; however, he was picked on constantly by the other two males and became the omega. Within five minutes of her encounter with the sibling males, female #511 had selected male wolf #509 as her mate.

"It was uncanny," Buchanan reported to Mike Taugher of the *Albuquerque Journal* for an April 1999 feature story, citing #511's speed in showing her preference. "She would always defend him. Ever since they have been together they are practically inseparable. They sleep next to each other. They are very compatible and a very strong pair." Buchanan went on to say, "She's amazing! I've seen a lot of wolves. You get to know when a wolf has it and when a wolf doesn't. She has it." In late April 1999, female #511 gave birth to four pups.

The third week in April, Buchanan, while working in the Blue, discovered that the Gavilan pack adult female #168 and her mate, #183, had produced five pups in the nylon-mesh acclimation pen near Coalson Peak. "I discovered that the female had dug out a southwest-facing shallow depression in the earth beneath a juniper tree." Buchanan reported that the pups looked to be about a week old at the time of her visit, and the family appeared to be doing well.

Because extremely dry conditions in the area had affected livestock distribution and their water sources, biologists decided to relocate the Gavilan pack to an area with less potential for conflict. On May 21, project personnel captured the three-member pack and their five six-week-old pups, four males and one female, and transported them several miles by helicopter to Horse Springs Canyon. There they were placed in a temporary nylon-mesh holding pen, and within twenty-four hours, they chewed out of the pen but remained in the area where they were supplementally fed and closely monitored.

Asher told me of a horseback trip she made in mid-April to monitor the activities of the Campbell Blue pair and to discuss her observations with a local rancher. "I saw the pair descending a steep ravine. Male wolf #166 saw me and immediately ran off, but female wolf #482 hesitated and just stared at me. I could hear the male whimpering farther up the trail. I threw rocks at #482 and yelled at her until she finally ran off."

A week later, another biologist was monitoring the same area and spied the Campbell Blue pair feeding on a fresh elk kill. Suddenly, the wolves got wind of his presence. Wolf #166 became nervous and ran off and #482 immediately followed. Asher said, "Determining the pregnancy of the free-ranging Campbell Blue pair, female #482 and male #166, is a tough call." She reported that the pair had localized their activities within a five-mile-square area, indicating that they might be tending a den.

The Hawk's Nest pair remained in their den throughout the early spring, with project personnel taking turns pen sitting. On May 13, Buchanan told Asher, "This morning I went out and found that female wolf #486 had three pups. I saw the alpha male wolf, #131, was standing close by." In early June, elk and new calves were observed in the area, and the Hawk's Nest pack was released. Project personnel provided supplemental road kill for the Hawk's Nest pack to meet the needs of the growing pups.

On May 22, 1999, the two four-year-old wolves from the Sevilleta wolf facility, male #190 and female #189, and their four six-week-old pups were driven to Alpine in trucks for their release. High winds greeted their arrival in Alpine, so the biologists held the wolves in crates overnight. Early the next morning they were flown by helicopter to a staging site outside of the Blue Range Primitive Area. From there, accompanied by project personnel riding mules, the wolves traveled in specially designed panniers, on mules, to a temporary mesh holding pen at Rousensock Creek. As Taylor related, "This was a landmark release because it was the first release site within the Blue Range Primitive Area and the first time wolves had ever been transported on mule back to their release site."

Appropriately, these wolves were named the Mule pack and were the first wolves anywhere to be transferred for release on the backs of mules. They chewed their way out of the nylon-mesh pen before the end of the next day. Biologists reported that the wolves were staying together in the release area, where they were closely monitored and supplementally fed until they started to kill their own food. By the end of July, the entire pack had crossed State Route 191 and traveled several miles to the Sheep Wash.

Dan Groebner, who helped the project personnel load the wolves on the long line under the helicopter for the first leg of the trip that eventually ended with the mule ride, was asked at an educators' workshop if the wolves had to be sedated. "No," Groebner replied. "We'd be given a supply of Valium for the wolves if they appeared stressed during their journey. Val Asher told me that once they settled down in their panniers, they were quite subdued." Groebner laughed, "Val had done such a good job in acclimating the mules before the trip by loading dogs in the panniers on test runs, that even the mules didn't need the Valium!"

During a mid-June telemetry flight over Four-Bar Mesa, biologists reported seeing two Pipestem wolves chasing an elk. When they returned the following day on foot, they could not find any signs of an elk kill, but they did find a dead domestic cow in a pasture, frequented by the Pipestem wolves, that was entangled in a barbed-wire fence. The biologists also found the remains of two calves in the same area and detected coyote and wolf signs near all three carcasses. There was not enough evidence left from the calves to ascertain the cause of death.

On June 18, while investigating the wolves' activities, Alan Armistead found pup scat and paw prints in the den drainage. It was later determined that the Pipestem female #191 had given birth to six pups.

On June 23, Asher called me to report a depredation had taken place on T-Links Ranch by the Pipestem pack, which had been confirmed the previous day by Alan Armistead. "The manager of the allotment called to report a female calf had been mauled," she said. "Alan believed that the wounds indicated more than one wolf by the location of bite marks in the shoulder and flank. The calf's wounds were cleaned, and antibiotics were administered. The calf was reunited with the mother and kept in a corral close to ranch headquarters." The calf made a full recovery.

On June 24, another dead calf was found, but its death was determined to be a lion kill. The next day biologists observed the Pipestem adults harassing a cow defending her calf and hazed the wolves from the area. On June 28, still another calf was found dead, almost completely consumed, leaving insufficient evidence for determining cause of death.

Defenders of Wildlife agreed to cover all of the veterinary expenses for the injured calf and also decided to pay compensation for the two dead calves, even though the scant remains made confirming the cause of their death impossible. The ranch manager seemed satisfied with the quick response to the wolf attack.

In reporting the calf attack to me, Asher said, "I am concerned about the behavior of the Pipestem pack after their continued altercations with the Dieringer cattle and dogs, as well as their cattle-chasing and the calf attack on the T-Links Ranch. I assigned project personnel to monitor the wolves' activities every four hours, night and day. If cattle losses continue, the Pipestem pack will have to be removed from the area."

Owing to the local reaction to the Pipestem pack's continued ranch interaction and wolf depredation, Parsons and Asher decided to postpone the return of female wolf #511 and her pack until the dismay over the Pipestem packs' behavior had quieted down. The Pipestem wolves sealed their fate the day one of the biologists observed them through binoculars turning up their noses at deer to run after cattle. "It was a tough call to make," admitted Groebner later to a July 1999 assemblage of Arizona educators, "but after considering all of the options, we decided to remove the Pipestem pack for the good of the recovery effort."

Groebner told the educators that they first considered other adaptive management options, including recapturing only the adult wolves but leaving the pups in the wild. They discarded this option because the pups were too young to survive on their own. Another option was to leave the Pipestem wolves in the forest and continue close monitoring with the hope that the wolves would alter their behavior. This option risked additional cattle kills that would tarnish the Mexican wolf program's image. Groebner said that they also considered a number of other options, including hazing the wolves away from the cattle, aversive taste conditioning, and livestock management. However, the drought that year limited flexibility in livestock management and neither hazing nor aversive conditioning had proven to be totally effective in the past. The biologists believed the best option was to recapture and return the pack to the Sevilleta wolf compound.

During July, project personnel placed elk meat inside the Turkey Creek acclimation pen to attract the wolves. When the alpha male went in after the meat, personnel quickly closed the inner gate behind him. They then placed meat in the outer entry area, and when the yearling female wolf tried to join her dad, they closed the outer gate after her. These two wolves were returned to Sevilleta.

Heavy monsoon rains in late July created muddy forest conditions that interrupted the recapture activity. Female wolf #191 was still lactating, and the biologists postponed capture of remaining pack members to avoid further trauma for the female, who was still nursing her pups.

Project personnel resumed recapture activity in mid-August. Two of the pups were captured and placed in the acclimation pen, while an attempt was made to capture the other pack members. On August 24, one of the captured pups, a male, was found dead from canine parvovirus, a contagious viral disease of both domestic and wild canines, usually fatal in young pups. Three more Pipestem pups were captured the same day, and the four pups were transported to Sevilleta.

Two more of the Pipestem pups died at Sevilleta from parvo. The other pups, although thin upon arrival, survived. All of the other pups at Sevilleta were captured and vaccinated for parvovirus. On September 7, two pups from captive female wolf #511 and male #509 were found dead of parvo at Sevilleta. Biologists were unable to locate the source of the viral disease in the Blue area, although it was suspected that campers' pet dogs may have infected the area.

During the next several weeks, the Pipestem female wolf was seen traveling with the sixth pup. No further cattle depredations by this female were reported. They were later recaptured and reunited with the remaining members of the Pipestem pack in Sevilleta.

Just before dawn, while I was camping at Luna Lake in late August with Jato, two wolves woke me from slumber with long sustained howls. I thanked God for letting me hear this song, because it announced that the essence of wildness had returned to the Blue. The birth of over a dozen new wolf pups had given the wolf recovery program an encouraging boost. The survival of these pups is the key to the program's success. The real proof of the success of the reintroduction effort will be achieved when wolves from the first healthy wild-born generation maintain themselves in the wild and produce pups in the Blue Range Area.

I admit to having a personal attachment to the Campbell Blue pair. Male #166, the wolf I had helped carry to his pen on January 1998, had been one of the two wolves who survived the massacre during 1998. Rosa's pup female #482 had been born following the construction of the improved breeding complex at the Phoenix Zoo, a project that P.A.WS. had initiated. Now this pair had bonded and may have produced pups that did not survive.

During the fall of 1999, Mike Seidman of the Phoenix Zoo told me something I had not known before. Jeff Williamson had named female wolf #482 Bobbie, after me. I can think of no greater honor. When I received my copy of the *1999 Mexican Wolf Stud Book* from Peter Siminski, of the ASDM, I found the name "Bobbie" listed with the data on female wolf #482. I called Siminski to thank him for mailing me the copy. He told me that during the spring of 1999, thirty-six pups had been born, with twenty-nine surviving in the captive facilities throughout the United States. Reports on this year's births from the facilities in Mexico as yet had not been received. Together with the wolves in the Blue, we had 210 Mexican wolves. When I recalled our concerns during the late 1980s, when only thirty Mexican wolves stood between the subspecies existence and extinction, 210 wolves represented a remarkable recovery.

By the end of 1999, more than twenty Mexican wolves roamed freely in the forests of the Blue Range Area. Despite desperate efforts made by wolf haters to slaughter all the wolves and bring an end to the program in 1998, it appeared that with the 1999 releases and births of pups, our Mexican wolves would survive and produce a viable population.

The lawsuit filed by the New Mexico Farm Bureau, the Cattle Growers, and others in March 1998 was dismissed in late 1999 because the judge determined that all of the allegations were invalid. This wise decision deprived the opposition of their last legal weapon against the return of the Mexican gray wolf back to the Blue.

16

From the Frontier to the Ecological Era

The polarization of wolf huggers and wolf haters was detrimental
to wolf conservation. There had to be some middle ground where
wolves and people could mutually exist, relatively free of conflicts.
—Diane Boyd-Heger, *Intimate Nature*

Some ranchers in the Blue Range Area wonder what happened
to all the lush grazing lands the old timers talked about. They
wonder why deer population numbers have so sharply declined.

When we read the history of the area, we learn of the literally thousands of cattle and sheep that grazed the area from the
1880s to the 1980s. In the beginning of the frontier era, during
the heyday of the cowboy, ranchers drove thousands of head
of cattle to market and were looked up to as paragons of success. It does not take an expert in range management to know
that unrestricted grazing of an area with thousands of head
of livestock for one hundred years will take its toll on vegetation, water sources, and soil conditions. Devastation of natural
resources resulted in lower deer populations. These populations
probably were also decreased by the import of elk, which com-
peted heavily with deer for forage. But none of this appears to
be readily apparent to the fourth- and fifth-generation ranchers
who are following the same patterns of grazing practiced by
their ancestors, who established homesteads in the area when
it was lush, green, and flowing with water. These ranchers har-
bor the hope that if they can just get rid of the Forest Service
regulations and the interference of the environmentalists, they

can return to the glory days of the cowboy that took place until the early twentieth century. This is not going to happen.

Today most public-land ranchers on forest land manage their allotments under a USFS Allotment Management Plan (AMP). Every ten years, these plans are reviewed by the Forest Service and the permittee to determine whether the allotment permit should be renewed. At one time, the Forest Service invited interested citizens to share in the scoping sessions on such AMPs, when a Forest Service–appointed interdisciplinary team discussed all phases of the allotment. Often such meetings involved tours of the allotment to consider soil and riparian conditions; I participated in many such meetings in the Prescott and Tonto National Forests. New grazing policies no longer allow public participation in these AMP meetings.

Many of the ranchers in the Blue Range Area have certain grandfathered rights because their ancestors homesteaded in the area long before the Forest Service was requiring AMPs. These ranchers operate with an Allotment Permit Issuance that is reviewed periodically and, in the past, was always reissued with little review of conditions or questions about grazing management. Because, in many cases, these ranchers' ancestors homesteaded the Blue country, it is difficult for them to accept the concept that they are actually leasing public land. It is easy to understand their dilemma after many generations have considered the land they use for their grazing operation as their land.

With the arrival of the Forest Service in the Blue Range Area, some ranchers resented having to pay annual fees for grazing on public land. As time went on, ranchers accepted the fee requirement, and most Forest Service range conservationists got along with the ranchers and seldom questioned their grazing methods. As late as the early 1990s, a range con named Gary Davis, who worked out of the Alpine District Forest Service, favored the ranchers and was well accepted. Davis was tragically killed in a plane crash in 1994 and was replaced with a range con named Mitchell White.

White had previously worked in Nevada, where he analyzed soil and water conditions on the various public-land allotments, and often recommended severe cuts in the numbers of cattle that ranchers were allowed to run. In the Alpine District, he was assigned the task of analyzing conditions on eight or nine of the allotments that still had Allotment Permit Issuance privileges that had gone unchallenged for years.

According to conversations I had with Don Hoffman of the Alpine District Forest Service, White did not base his analysis on ecological criteria or on threats to endangered or threatened species, but rather used standard range-management principles. He conducted studies on these allotments to determine the livestock capacity of the land based on soil and range science. All lands having more than a 40 percent slope and that were one-quarter mile or more from a water source were considered unavailable when calculating the range capacity. This is based on the theory that before livestock would utilize these areas, unacceptable damage already would have occurred within the sensitive riparian corridors. Because much of the Blue Range Area consists of steep canyons with rivers or streams at the bottom, this analysis cut many acres from the lands previously used to calculate capacity. Much of the suitable land consisted of narrow riparian areas bordering the rivers and streams. As a result, the recommendations in White's analysis called for drastic cuts in animal unit months (AUMs), which on some allotments decreased livestock numbers by 80 percent.

When word of White's recommendations reached the ranchers' ears, they were furious over what they referred to as his "hatchet jobs" on their AUM numbers. White left his position as the Alpine District's range con and was replaced by Buck McKinney, who had formerly worked in the Tonto National Forest. McKinney enforced White's recommendations. There might

have been some modifications to the range-management criteria used to determine suitable numbers, but the cuts in cattle
numbers remained quite severe. The ranchers of the Greenlee
County Cattle Growers Association got together and filed a
lawsuit against the Forest Service over this matter, but to my
knowledge, this litigation has never been settled.

To further add to the ranchers' wrath, the USFWS discovered that the Blue River, and other riparian areas in the Blue,
contained endangered fish, such as the loach minnow and the
spike dace. The endangered willow flycatcher made its home
along these same riparian areas. The Southwest Center for Biodiversity had filed a lawsuit over the fact that continued grazing in these riparian areas was detrimental to these and other
endangered species. The Forest Service settled the lawsuit without litigation by requiring ranchers to fence off all riparian areas
and remove the cattle from stream and river beds. This left little
suitable land for the ranchers, who felt that their embattled
position was hopeless. Some, like Tim and Dink Robarts, sold
out and gave up ranching.

Hershel Downs was a rancher on eighty square miles of
national forest in the Blue for nearly fifty years. White's recommendations cut Downs's numbers from 225 to 46. Blue ranchers affected by the proposed cuts believed that the future for
grazing cattle in the area was bleak, and predicted that the
Forest Service would phase out ranching in the area and let the
Blue River country revert to pristine wildlife habitat. Many of
them sold their leases and pursued other livelihoods.

Barbara and Billy Marks succeeded in maintaining their grazing operation when they agreed to a Forest Service AMP. They
took a cut in cattle numbers, but Billy Marks worked on local
road maintenance, in addition to his ranch work, to bring in
enough funds to provide a living for his family.

Don Hoffman told me that the recovery in areas of the Blue
affected by the removal of cattle was remarkable. Willow growth

rapidly took place along the Blue River, and other plant regrowth was noticeable in several riparian areas. The Hoffmans, who had made the Blue River country their home since 1977, welcomed this restoration of the riparian system.

Many of the ranchers affected by the cuts were among the most strident opposers of the return of the wolf, blaming the evil beast for putting them out of business, and blaming environmentalists for being insensitive to their customs and culture. Wolf hatred is not limited to the confines of the Blue area. The capitol chapter of the People for the USA (formerly People for the West) advertised their March 4, 1999, Phoenix meeting as follows:

Arizona's Wolf Infestation

If you make one meeting, let this be the one. Charles Erickson of the Arizona Beef Council will talk about the wolf infestation in Eastern Arizona and how the Endangered Species Act is being used by environmental activists to end Arizona's cattle industry. The tools and tactics of these green terrorists were developed and proven in the war on logging in the West. The greens won. Now these same groups and individuals are focusing on the cattle growers. When they have eliminated ranching they will focus on mining. You will be next.

These tactics echo those used in prewar Germany when the green uniformed soldiers of Hitler's Third Reich isolated groups of people for neutralization.

Despite this extreme rhetoric, forest managers must take action to preserve public-land wildlife habitat for all species, plant and animal. Even with the drastic reductions in cattle numbers, the land may not fully recover. If there is any hope for even a partial recovery to what the Blue Range Area was in the 1880s, land managers must make every attempt to achieve whatever restoration is possible.

Survey upon survey has revealed overwhelming public support for healthy wildlife populations. Scientists have proved that healthy wildlife populations mean a healthy ecosystem, but no wildlife population missing a major species can be considered healthy. As has been illustrated in Yellowstone, the greater the diversity of wildlife, the greater are the probabilities for an ecosystem to rebound. In the Blue, the return of the top predator, in this case the Mexican wolf, can achieve the full complement of wildlife that the forest and all of its residents deserve. What greater legacy can we leave to future generations than a heritage of pristine forests with healthy and diverse wildlife populations?

In contrast to ranchers who vilify both the Mexican wolf and the advocates that support its return, it has been rewarding to see the efforts being made by more progressive ranchers who support wolf recovery. Will and Jan Holder, who operate the Anchor Ranch along Eagle Creek, manage their allotment with tolerance toward all predators, including wolves. Will Holder goes out early every morning to move his cattle to prevent overgrazing of plants and to avoid predation.

The Holders told me that their Ervin's Natural Beef business is still growing as they expand into several health-food stores. Alaine Ducasse, noted French chef, upon hearing about the Holders's organically produced beef, traveled to Eagle Creek, where Jan prepared a savory tenderloin beef dinner for him. Jan told me he said it was the finest beef he had ever tasted. He included Ervin's Natural Beef in his book *Harvesting Excellence,* chronicling the best organic products in the world, and serves Ervin's Natural Beef at his exclusive Essex House restaurant in New York City.

As an effort to diversify their revenue base, the Holders are sponsoring El Rancho Lobo tours, on which participants can visit wolf habitat and learn about livestock management that respects all wildlife species. Since switching from a cow-calf to

a yearling operation, the Holders also bring along a few paying
guests as roundup cowboys on their four-day annual trail ride
to drive the stockers from the San Carlos Apache Reservation to
Anchor Ranch.

Clarice Holder, Will's mother, gave me permission to include
portions of her unpublished article, explaining her perspective
of why some of today's ranchers think the way they do:

> What wrong turn did ranchers make to go from being folk-
> lore heroes to becoming the bad guys?
>
> As ranchers, we did not realize that our ranching prac-
> tices were affecting the land. It either rained or it didn't,
> that is what affected the land, it wasn't anything that we
> did or did not do.
>
> How we ranch, unfortunately, definitely affects the land
> and we are probably to blame for a lot of the problems
> that we now have. The thought is so unacceptable to us as
> ranchers that we can't believe we could have done any-
> thing so horrible.
>
> Ranchers have been taught to manage for cattle and
> cattle only. The top priority was the weaning weight of the
> calves if it was a cow/calf operation.... We knew about
> implants to get bigger weaning weights and preventative
> measures to use such as vaccines, dips, and sprays to pre-
> vent flies and grubs. From our ranching family we learned
> how to brand, rope, ride, drive cattle, and all the other
> multitude of tasks. Great pride was taken in these skills,
> and great fun was poked at any newcomer (dude); envi-
> ronmentalists definitely fall under this category.
>
> When the environmentalists told the ranchers what a
> terrible thing they were doing to the land, even the thought
> threw the rancher into complete culture shock. How could
> anyone listen to such complete garbage? Couldn't they see
> that the rancher loved his land? Didn't they realize how
> foolish such remarks like that were? Of course, we loved
> this land. We and our families have been here for genera-
> tions.... We knew how to ranch; what could these new-
> comers tell us?

The whole idea has thrown the entire cattle industry into such a shock that it is much easier to deny than it has been to start looking at the land and wondering where to go from here. Some of the ranching community have finally come out of shock and are trying to help heal the land but other groups continue to deny there are any problems. Unfortunately, most cattle organizations are spending much time, money, and energy trying to defend the image of the rancher from the past.

Environmentalists are beginning to realize they do not have all the answers. The environmental community would be more productive if they would stop pointing fingers and begin to work with the ranching community.

Is there hope for the ranching community? That will depend upon the ranchers themselves. Ranchers must accept the fact that times have changed and we must also change with the times looking to the future with new inventive ideas. Let's all join to protect and enhance today's environment even it if means giving up the past as we once knew it to be. It is no more and never will be, no matter how hard we struggle to prevent change. We must not manage for one species—cattle. The land, domesticated animals, other diverse ungulates, and wildlife species go together. Each species belongs with the others.

We will never realize recovery of the forest lands and a full complement of wildlife in the Blue unless we are willing to reach out and understand the people who live there. This is going to require open minds and cooperative efforts with ranchers and other local citizens. It will require collaborative interaction; it will not happen by filing a rash of lawsuits.

It is far too easy for city dwellers to criticize ranchers' practices, and to look with unsympathetic eyes on the problems that confront them as they bridge the transition between the cowboy's frontier era and the future's ecological era. As seen by realistic scientists like Diane Boyd-Heger, who faced everyday interaction with ranchers who opposed the return of wolves, it

Refuge in Minnesota. Naftal reported that the local opposition to Mexican wolves has eased among Arizona ranchers, but in New Mexico, ranchers retain their violent hatred of wolves.

Naftal was assisted by Alexis Watts, who had been working for several months on the project as a biotech. Watts earned her bachelor's degree in biology at Carlton College in Minnesota, and a master's degree in wildlife biology at Utah State University.

Early in 2001, Wendy Brown left the Mexican wolf program. The USFWS hired Dan Stark as a biotech for the Mexican wolf program to work out of their field office in Glenwood, New Mexico. Stark graduated from St. Cloud University in Minnesota with a bachelor's degree in wildlife biology and later worked on David Mech's wolf projects in northern Minnesota.

According to the March 10, 2000, article by Judd Slivka of the *Arizona Republic,* James Michael Rogers of Eagar was arrested on charges of killing female wolf #493 of the Hawk's Nest pack in October 1998. Rogers, 21, admitted to authorities that he had lied thirteen months earlier when questioned by authorities concerning the killing. Despite the early testimony, authorities continued investigating him, focusing on activities of Rogers and his cousin, Edward Rogers, 19, also of Eagar. When confronted with the federal investigators' evidence, James Rogers admitted that he shot the wolf near Nutrioso, and then carried the carcass to New Mexico to conceal its death. The USFWS did not reveal the source of the evidence that led to the arrest.

Because the younger Edward had been a juvenile, court documents relating to his role in the killing were sealed. Upon arraignment in federal court in Flagstaff, James Rogers pleaded innocent. At his court hearing on May 17, 2000, he was indicted for killing an endangered Mexican wolf. On October 20, 2000, he was sentenced to four months in prison, six months of house arrest, and fifty hours of community service. Federal authorities are still looking for information that would lead to the arrest of the killers of the other wolves that were illegally shot.

Campbell Blue Pack

For a few months, the alpha male wolf, #166, roamed the woods with the two female offspring of his fourth mate, #522. His second mate, female wolf #482, was found dead on October 27, 1999, near State Route 191. This was the wolf named Bobbie, and my only consolation was that the necropsy report indicated she died from a lion kill and not from a human killer's gunshot. Female wolf #522 was transferred from Ladder Ranch as a new mate for #166 early in 2000. After release from the Engineer Spring acclimation pen, she pursued hunting dogs and later a rancher's dogs and was returned to captivity. A month later, a new mate, female wolf #519, with her two yearling female pups, #592 and #594, were placed in Engineer Spring pen. Male wolf #166 was seen waiting outside the pen before the pen was opened. After release, #519 and her pups bonded with #166 and for a time traveled as a pack. When female wolf #519 harassed a rancher's dogs in the Eagle Creek area in April 2000, she was captured and returned to Sevilleta. Male wolf #166 continued to travel with the two yearling female offspring.

Female wolf #594 dispersed from the other two wolves and traveled west towards Flagstaff. On October 7, 2000, female wolf #594 was hit and killed by a passing vehicle east of Flagstaff on State Highway 89.

Following complaints from the San Carlos Apache Reservation, where male wolf #166 and female wolf #592 were observed, biologists captured the two wolves and placed them in the Engineer Spring pen before returning them to the Sevilleta facility. Female wolf #592 suffered a leg injury when trying to dig out of the enclosure but later made a full recovery. On December 20, the pair was released near Tom Moore Mesa in the Gila National Forest of New Mexico, and after a few weeks they separated and traveled separately for several months. Early in May 2001, the pair was observed together by a local rancher and during June by biologists, who hoped their reunion would indicate they had finally bonded.

Hawk's Nest Pack

Alpha male #131, alpha female #486, and their pups, wolves #600, #601, and #602, remained together and successfully killed native prey for food. During the spring of 2000, the alpha pair produced a litter of pups.

On October 26, 2000, Alexis Watts encountered alpha male #131 appearing disoriented. She captured him and took him to a veterinary clinic for examination. The vet treated the wolf for infection, but his condition worsened, and on November 1, wolf #131 was euthanized. Necropsy results showed that he was suffering from an incurable brain tumor and had sustained several broken ribs and a fractured leg from elk hunting. Male wolf #131 was one of the two remaining males from the 1998 release and was an extremely successful pack leader. He and his second mate produced the only pup in 1999 that remains free ranging, and they produced male pup #674 in 2000. The Hawk's Nest pack had never been involved in livestock depredation.

Female wolf #486 and male wolf #674 continued to move primarily within their usual territory around the Campbell Blue and Beaver Creek drainages in Arizona's Apache National Forest in the Hawk's Nest territory. Early in 2001, female wolf #486 bonded with Cienega pack male wolf #619. (The Cienega pack was formed by wolves from Wolf Haven in Washington, introduced in 2000 to the northern Blue Range Area.) This male wolf replaced wolf #131 as the Hawk's Nest alpha male and was no longer considered a member of the Cienega pack. In April 2001, male wolf #674 was observed exploring the forest with female wolf #587 of the Francisco pack (descendants of Campbell Blue female #511 and male #509).

Gavilan Pack

The Alpha male, #183, alpha female, #168, yearling male, #555, and pups—male wolves #582, #583, #584, and #586, and female wolf #585—traveled as a pack throughout the lower Blue. They attacked cattle that were grazing illegally, having crossed their allotment boundary because of unmended broken fences. After several cattle were severely wounded and one killed, the entire Gavilan pack was pushed, by Mexican wolf project staff, north to the Maple Peak area.

They later traveled over the New Mexico border, and having acquired a taste for beef, some members of the pack again depredated livestock. The decision was made to recapture the entire pack and remove them from the forest. Yearling male wolf #555 eluded capture and remained free in the wilds of the Gila National Forest for many months. Field personnel witnessed him attacking a cow elk, but before the death of the elk could be confirmed, the yearling moved off.

In February 2000, a rancher near where wolf #555 last had been seen reported that a cow in the O Bar O Canyon had been bitten around the ears, head, and tail. Alan Armistead could not confirm that the wolf had been involved, and the cow recovered from the injuries. There have been no further sightings by monitoring field staff of male wolf #555. His disappearance signaled the end of the Gavilan pack.

Pipestem Pack

In December 1999, alpha female wolf, #191, and pup #628 were captured near Engineer Spring in the Strayhorse area and reunited with the alpha male wolf, #208, and surviving pups, female #624 and male #627, at Sevilleta. All wolves were in good health and considered candidates for re-release.

In early April 2000, the alpha pair, male wolf #208 and female wolf #191, and their three pups—females #624 and #628 and male #627—were transported by mules to a mesh pen in the Halfmoon Park area in the Gila Wilderness. On April 15, field personnel opened the gate of the pen, and for a few weeks, the pack remained near the release pen. The alpha female, #191, was pregnant at the time of the transfer. In late April, female #624 was located approximately twenty miles away from her pack on Forest Service land near Alma, New Mexico, and later moved into Arizona and was located south of Springerville for several days before moving outside of the recovery area. In July, the biologists recaptured her and returned her to captivity in the Sevilleta facility.

The alpha female, #191, gave birth to an undetermined number of pups in early June 2000, and she remained at her den tending the pups while other remaining pack members dispersed.

On June 16, 2000, the alpha male, #208, and other pack members were encountered in Gila Hot Springs. The alpha male was trapped and removed to prevent him from leading the pack into a populated area. The female wolf #628 rejoined her mother, female wolf #191, but the male wolf #627 ran off and was last located near Silver City, New Mexico, on July 2, 2000. The biologists received no signal from that wolf after that date. In August, female #191 and female #628 separated for a short period but later reunited. They were observed traveling with Mule pack male wolf #190 on the middle fork of the Gila River. On April 24, 2001, female wolf #191 was found dead, apparently from natural causes, while male wolf #190 assumed lead role for the Pipestem pack.

Mule Pack

Alpha male, #190, alpha female, #189, and pups—males #578, #580, and #581, and female #579—adjusted to the wild but continued to receive supplemental feedings. They moved into the Eagle Creek area where there are many deer. In late fall 1999, Jan Holder reported that an old horse belonging to the Fillaman Ranch was dying in the middle of the forest road leading from her house to State Route 191. She offered to help remove the horse to clear the road. Before action could be taken, the horse died, and the Mule pack was seen by other local ranchers eating the carcass. Frantic calls to the Alpine Mexican wolf project office reported that the wolves had killed the horse. The decision was made by project personnel to recapture the Mule pack and move them from the Eagle Creek area. In the process, the alpha female was left in a leg-hold trap in freezing temperatures, and one front leg had to be amputated. The pack, minus pups female #579 and male #581, was returned to Sevilleta while the female recovered from the surgery. The two missing pups were assumed by project personnel to be dead.

In March 2000, with the three-legged alpha female, #189, now pregnant, the Mule pack was transferred into a mesh pen in Creel Canyon near Lily Park in the Gila Wilderness. They broke out of the pen in a few days and explored the area. In April 2000, the alpha male and two yearlings, male wolves #578 and #580, headed out of the wilderness towards the town of Cliff, New Mexico. In April, field staff trapped the three males and returned them to Sevilleta.

On June 6, 2000, the alpha male, #190, was reunited with female #189 and their new pups, while their yearling male wolves remained at Sevilleta.

In September 2000, the alpha male left the female and was located in the middle fork of the Gila River with the Pipestem females. The alpha female, #189, moved to the Blue River on the west end of Alma Mesa. During November 2000, the female moved back into her original area, near Four-Bar Mesa in Arizona. There has been no sign of female wolf #189 since February 2001, and she is assumed dead.

Cienega Pack

On March 13, 2000, alpha male, #194, alpha female, #487, and yearling pups male #619, female #620, and female #621 were flown from Wolf Haven in Washington and transported on mules to a soft mesh pen near Steeple Creek in the northern Blue Range Area. These wolves were named the Cienega pack after the nearby riparian drainage. After escape from the mesh pen, male wolf pup #620 was killed by a car on State Route 191 near Hannagan Meadow.

The pack traveled to Hannagan Meadow and K P Creek, where collected scat indicated that the pack had successfully killed elk. Supplemental feeding was discontinued.

In November 2000, the pack moved from the Hannagan area to Beaver Creek. The alpha pair, male wolf #194 and female wolf #487, returned to Hannagan and then moved to the Steeple Creek Mesa. The two yearlings, male wolf #619 and female wolf #621, traveled separately. In December, male wolf #619, now nearly two years old, went to Williams Valley and Coyote Creek and joined the Hawk's Nest female #486. Female wolf #621 was located in December, exploring Escudilla Mountain alone. In March 2001, she rejoined her parents near the Blue Vista.

Francisco Pack

The Campbell Blue female #511 mated with male wolf #509 at Sevilleta, and during 1999 produced four pups in captivity, two of which died from parvovirus. The pair produced four more pups in the spring of 2000. On July 13, 2000, the alpha pair, their two yearlings, female wolf #587 and male wolf #590, and four pups—males #641, #642, and #643, and female #644— were placed into a mesh pen in the remote Bear Wallow Wilderness and were called the Francisco pack.

The pack soon exhibited their ability to kill elk, and all eight members of the pack were observed traveling together. On October 13, they were located in Conklin Creek with the Cienega Pack. On November 26, male wolf #590 moved across the Blue River and was located a few miles northwest of Reserve, New Mexico. On or about December 16, he was shot and killed near Reserve. Federal authorities offered a $10,000 reward for apprehension of the killer. The remaining pack members, including pups born in spring of 2001 to the alpha pair, have been located moving between Bear Wallow Wilderness and the Black River on the San Carlos Apache Reservation. During April 2001, female wolf #587 was observed with Hawk's Nest male wolf #674.

Saddle Pack

On January 3, 2001, a pack of six wolves consisting of the alpha male, #574, female wolf #510, and their four pups—females #645 and #646 and males #647 and #648—were placed in the Engineer Spring acclimation pen. The wolves were named the Saddle pack and were the first to be released carrying the Aragon lineage through the alpha male. The alpha female is one of the captive-bred offspring of the former free-ranging Mule pack adults.

Because heavy snow fell following the wolves' placement in the pen, the biologists released the pack earlier than anticipated after only one week of acclimation. The pack explored nearby creeks near Chitty Canyon. Male wolf #647 was later located on the White Mountain Apache Reservation and male wolf #648 explored areas on the San Carlos Apache Reservation.

Wildcat Pack

On March 17, 2001, former Pipestem pack female #624 and former Mule pack males #578 and #580 were transported from the Sevilleta facility to a remote area north of the Black River near

Wildcat Creek. The pack was released immediately and given the name of nearby Wildcat Creek. Biologists reported that they suspected the female had already been bred by one of the males that had shared the pen with her in Sevilleta. Initially, the pack stayed together near the Black River but later dispersed and widely explored the surrounding territory. During March 2001, female wolf #624 was located near Beaverhead, New Mexico, while male wolf #578 moved into the Gila Wilderness of New Mexico. Male wolf #580 was located south of the Blue Vista in Arizona.

Lupine Pack

On June 18, 2001, project staff members transferred nine wolves from the Ladder Ranch facility to Alpine, Arizona. The next day, the pack, named the Lupine pack, was placed in mesh pens in the Bear Wallow area, about twenty miles southwest of Alpine. The alpha male, #480, born at the Phoenix Zoo in 1996, was the brother of female wolf #482, killed by a mountain lion in October 1999, the former mate of the Campbell Blue alpha male, #166. The alpha female wolf, #169, was born at the Wild Canid Survival and Research Center in Eureka, Missouri, in 1994. In spring of 2000, the pair produced four pups, male wolves #630, #632, and #634, and female wolf #631. About eight weeks before their release, the alpha pair produced three additional pups.

Bonita Creek Pack

Former Hawk's Nest pack male wolf #674 and Francisco pack female wolf #587 continued to travel together and were given the name Bonita Creek pack from the Big Bonita Lake, where they were first located. They remained near that area for several weeks before moving southeast to Reservation Lake on the White Mountain Apache Reservation.

By mid-summer 2001, nearly forty wolves in ten packs roamed the forests in the Apache and Gila National Forests. Of the original eleven released in January 1998, only two survived in the wild: Campbell Blue pack alpha male wolf #166 and his then-yearling "poster wolf" female #511, now the alpha female of the Francisco pack.

According to Peter Siminski, keeper of the *Mexican Wolf Stud Book,* the official 2000 year-ending population of all Mexican wolves, including those free in the Blue Range Area and in forty-seven captive facilities, was 214. In June 2001, project biologists from the Alpine office reported that pups had been born to four or five packs, but they were unable to determine the number of pups in each litter. The total Mexican wolf population may be augmented by thirty or more when all of the breeding facilities in the United States and Mexico report on Mexican wolf pups born in spring 2001.

Despite early setbacks, the Mexican wolf program is on the road to achieving its goal of one hundred wolves in the Blue Range Area. With more human tolerance and less human intervention, our Mexican gray wolves brought back to the Blue will thrive.

Sources and Suggested Reading

Readers may wish to obtain two maps from the U.S. Forest Service in order to locate the areas mentioned in the text: the Apache-Sitgreaves National Forests map and the Blue Range Wilderness and Primitive Area map showing Arizona and New Mexico. The maps may be purchased from Apache Sitgreaves National Forests, P.O. Box 640, 309 South Mountain Avenue, Springerville, AZ 85938.

Abbey, Edward. *Beyond the Wall.* New York: Holt, Rinehart and Winston, 1971.

Alderton, David. *Foxes, Wolves and Wild Dogs of the World.* New York: Blandford, of Cassell, Facts on File, 1994.

American Hunter. "Wolf Investigation Raises Ire of Hunters." (March 1999):7

Arizona Cattle Growers Association (AGCA). "Resolutions of the AGCA Adopted at the 88th Annual Convention August 1991, Tucson, Arizona." *Cattlelog* (September–October):28–35.

Arizona Game and Fish Commission. *Comment on U.S. Fish and Wildlife Service Draft Environmental Impact Statement on Mexican Wolf Reintroduction into the Southwest.* Phoenix: Arizona Game and Fish Department, 1995.

———. *Mexican Wolf DEIS-Commissioner by Mike Golightly's Motion.* Phoenix: Arizona Game and Fish Department, 1995.

Arizona Game and Fish Department. *Procedures for Nongame Wildlife and Endangered Species Re-Establishment Projects in Arizona.* Phoenix: Arizona Game and Fish Department, 1987. (Includes the Arizona 12-Step procedure.)

———. "Public Opinion Survey of Arizona Residents and Interest Groups about the Mexican Wolf." Phoenix: Arizona Game and Fish Department, 1990.

———. *Summary of Information on Four Potential Mexican Wolf Reintroduction Areas in Arizona.* Technical Report 23. Phoenix: Arizona Game and Fish Department, 1992.

———. *Mexican Wolf Surveys and Arizona and Mexico.* In cooperation with U.S. Fish and Wildlife Service and Proteccion de la Fauna Mexicana A.C. Phoenix: Arizona Game and Fish Department, 1995.

———. *A Proposed Cooperative Reintroduction Plan for the Mexican Wolf in Arizona*. Technical Report 56. Phoenix: Arizona Game and Fish Department, 1995.

———. *Memorandum of Understanding among U.S. Fish and Wildlife Service and Arizona Game and Fish Department*. Phoenix: Arizona Game and Fish Department, 1997.

Askins, Renee. "Releasing Wolves from Symbolism." Congressional Testimony. New York: *Harpers Magazine* (April 1995):15–17.

Associated Press. "Agency Retreats on Wolf Questionnaire." *The Arizona Republic*, 20 December 1998.

Bagwell, Keith. "Three Mexican Gray Wolves to Be Released in Arizona Today." *The Arizona Daily Star*, 26 January 1998, 1A–3A.

Bass, Rick. *The New Wolves*. New York: The Lyons Press, 1998.

Bednarz, James C. *The Mexican Wolf: Biology, History, and Prospects for Reestablishment in New Mexico*. Albuquerque, N.Mex.: U.S. Fish and Wildlife Service, 1988.

———. *An Evaluation of the Ecological Potential of White Sands Missile Range to Support a Reintroduced Population of Mexican Wolves*. Albuquerque, N.Mex.: U.S. Fish and Wildlife Service, 1989.

Bodfield, Rhonda. "Wolf Killings Upset U.S., but Alpine Growls Back." *Tucson Citizen*, 15 November 1998, 1A.

Bomford, Liz. *The Complete Wolf*. New York: St. Martin's Press, 1993.

Bowden, Charles. "Will the Wolf Dance in Arizona Again?" *Phoenix* (October 1991):86–91.

———. "Lonesome Lobo." *Wildlife Conservation* (January/February 1992): 44–53, 73.

Boyd-Heger, Diane. "Living with Wolves." From *Intimate Nature*, edited by Brenda Peterson et al., 90–96. New York: Fawcett Columbine, 1998.

Brown, David E. *The Wolf in the Southwest*. Tucson: The University of Arizona Press, 1984.

———. "Wildlife Commission Confused about Role, Unsure about Funding." *The Arizona Republic*, 5 October 1988.

———. "Lobo." *Audubon* (January 1990):17–18.

———. "Wolves Need Human Allies to Make Restoration Successful." *High Country News*, 23 April 1990, 6.

Burbank, James C. *Vanishing Lobo*. Boulder, Colo.: Johnson Publishing Co., 1990.

Busch, Robert H. *The Wolf Almanac*. New York: Lyons & Burford, 1995.

Caras, Roger A. *The Custer Wolf*. Lincoln: The University of Nebraska Press, 1990.

The Coronado Trail Parkway: An Early Alpine History. N.p., n.d.

Crane, Candace. "The Last of the Lobos." *Animals* (July/August 1989):18–24.

———. "The Wolf Lady." *Animals* (January/February 1996):32–33.

Erickson, Jim. "Gray Wolves Unafraid of Man, Campers Say." *The Arizona Daily Star,* 1 May 1998, B1.

Fischer, Hank. *Wolf Wars.* Helena, Mont.: Falcon Press Publishing Co., 1995.

Flader, Susan L. *Thinking Like a Mountain: Aldo Leopold and the Evolution of an Ecological Attitude Toward Deer, Wolves, and Forests.* Columbia, Mo.: The University of Missouri Press, 1974.

Fox, Michael W. *Behavior of Wolves, Dogs and Related Canids.* New York: Harper & Row, 1971.

——— *The Soul of the Wolf.* Boston: Little, Brown & Co., 1980.

Garcia-Moreno, Jaime, Marjorie D. Matocq, Michael S. Roy, Eli Geffen, and Robert K. Wayne. "Relationships and Genetic Purity of the Endangered Mexican Wolf Based on Analysis of Microsatellite Loci." *Conservation Biology* 10 (1996):376–89.

Gibson, Nancy. *Wolves.* Stillwater, Minn.: Voyageur Press, 1996.

Gish, Dan Miles. *An Historical Look at the Mexican Gray Wolf* (Canis lupus baileyi) *in Early Arizona Territory and Since Statehood.* Albuquerque, N.Mex.: U.S. Fish and Wildlife Service, 1977.

Greeley, Maureen. *Wolf.* New York: Friedman/Fairfax Publishers, 1996.

Grooms, Steve. *The Return of the Wolf.* Minocqua, Wis.: NorthWord Press, 1993.

Hedrick, Philip W., and Genetics Committee of the Mexican Wolf Recovery Team. "Genetic Evaluation of the Three Captive Mexican Wolf Lineages and Consequent Recommendations." Department of Zoology, Arizona State University (1995):1–23.

Hedrick, Philip W., Philip S. Miller, Eli Geffen, and Robert Wayne. "Genetic Evaluation of the Three Captive Mexican Wolf Lineages." *Zoo Biology* 16 (1997):47–67.

Holaday, Bobbie. "The Mexican Gray Wolf—Will We Permit Its Return?" *Arizona Wildlife News* (January 1992):7.

———. "Wolf Letter to Editor." *Arizona Wildlife News* (March 1992):11.

———. "Will We Bring Back the Mexican Wolf?" *Howler* (Spring 1994):4–5.

———. "Setting the Stage for Release of Mexican Wolves in 1998." *Wolf! Magazine* (Summer 1997):1.

———. "USFWS Lets Wolf Killer Off Scot Free." *Wolf! Magazine* (Spring/Summer 1998):7.

Holaday, Bobbie, ed. *PAW PRINTS,* November 1989–August 1998. (Newsletter of Preserve Arizona's Wolves; source of history of P.A.WS.'s activities.)

Hughes, Stella. *Hashknife Cowboy.* Tucson and London: The University of Arizona Press, 1984.

Hunger, Kate. "Ranchers Angry, Babbitt Upbeat Over Lobo Release." *Arizona Daily Sun,* 27 January 1998, 1, 8.

International Union for Conservation of Nature. *Captive Breeding Specialist Group, Population Viability Analysis for the Mexican Wolf Workshop Briefing Document.* Apple Valley, Minn.: IUCN, 1990.

———. *Mexican Wolf Population Biology and Simulation Modeling.* Apple Valley, Minn.: IUCN, 1996.

Johnson, Aubrey Stephen. "Will Lobo Come Home?" *Defenders* (January/ February: 1991):10–17.

Johnson, Nonie, Chair, AGF Commission. Letter to Nancy Kaufman, Director, Region 2, USFWS. Public Records (January 1997): 1.

Lawrence, R.D. *Trail of the Wolf.* Emmaus, Penn.: Rodale Press, 1993.

Leopold, Aldo. *A Sand County Almanac.* New York: Oxford University Press, 1949.

Lopez, Barry. *Of Wolves and Men.* New York: Scribner, 1978.

Lopez, Sonny. "Cruces Wolf Hearing Becomes Heckling Match." *Las Cruces Journal,* 27 February 1991.

Marks, Barbara. "Arizona Ranch Families in Search of the Truth about Wolves." A Press Release from the Arizona Beef Council/Arizona Cattlemen's Association (December 1998).

McBride, Roy T. *The Mexican Wolf: A Historical Review and Observations on Its Status and Distribution.* Albuquerque, N.Mex.: U.S. Department of the Interior Fish and Wildlife Service, 1980.

McClain, Carla. "Three Gray Wolves Released in Arizona Wilds." *Tucson Citizen,* 27 January 1998, 1A, 6A.

———. "Cover-up Alleged in Shooting of Wolf." *Tucson Citizen,* 16 June 1998, 1A.

———. "Rewards Boosting Info on Wolf Killers." *Tucson Citizen,* 15 November 1998.

McIntyre, Rick. *A Society of Wolves.* Stillwater, Minn.: Voyageur Press, 1993.

———. *War Against the Wolf.* Stillwater, Minn.: Voyageur Press, 1995.

McNamee, Thomas. *The Return of the Wolf to Yellowstone.* New York: Henry Holt and Company, 1997.

Mech, L. David. *The Wolf: The Ecology and Behavior of an Endangered Species.* Minneapolis: University of Minnesota Press, 1970.

———. *The Way of the Wolf.* Stillwater, Minn.: Voyageur Press, 1991.

Minclier, Kit. "Arizonans Feel Threatened by Wolf Release." *Denver Post,* 1 February 1998, B2.

Moody, Joan. "El Lobo's Homecoming." *Defenders* (Spring 1998):6–9.

Morgan, Anne Hodges, and Rennard Strickland, eds. *Arizona Memories.* Tucson: The University of Arizona Press, 1984.

Murr, Andrew. "Deadly Days for Wolves." *Newsweek,* 30 November 1998, 34.

Nelson, Ray. "El Lobo's Return." *New Mexico Magazine* (January 1999): 20–24.

O'Driscoll, Patrick. "Cry of Wolf Returning to Southwest." *USA Today,* 27 January 1998, 8A.

Parker, Dennis. "Southwest Wolves: Discussion of Their Taxonomical Arrangement, an Examination of the Ancestry of Captive-Bred Lines and A Current Field Investigation Pertaining to the Status of the Mexican Gray Wolf *(Canis lupus baileyi)* in Southeastern Arizona." Patagonia, Ariz.: privately printed paper, 1987.

———. "A Reader's Response on Reintroduction." *Arizona Wildlife News* (February 1992):7, 10.

———. "Mexican Wolves—The Debate Continues." *Arizona Wildlife News* (April 1992):3.

———. *Reintroduction of the Mexican Wolf: Instrument of Recovery or Instrument of Demise?* Patagonia, Ariz.: Applied Ecosystem Management, 1995.

Parsons, David R., compiler. *A Critical Review of an Unpublished, Undated Paper by Dennis Parker (Biologist, Applied Ecosystem Management, Inc.) Titled Reintroduction of the Mexican Wolf: Instrument of Recovery or Instrument of Demise?* Albuquerque, N.Mex.: U.S. Fish and Wildlife Service, 1995.

Phillips, Michael K., and Douglas W. Smith. *The Wolves of Yellowstone.* Stillwater, Minn.: Voyageur Press, 1996.

Preserve Arizona's Wolves and Arizona Wildlife Society. *Proceedings from Arizona Wolf Symposium '90.* Phoenix: privately printed, 1990.

Rosas, Octavio C. *"El Lobo Gris en el Noreste de Mexico: Un Caso para Reflexionar."* *Dumac* (January 1997):24–27.

Ruger, Lynn. *Mileposts along the Coronado Trail Scenic Byway.* N.p., 1994.

Savage, Harlin. "Waiting for El Lobo." *Defenders* (Fall 1995):8–15.

Savory, Allan. *Holistic Resource Management.* Covelo, Calif.: Island Press, 1988.

Siminski, D. Peter. "Mexican Wolf SSP Status Report." AZA National Conference, Atlanta, Ga., 1994.

Slivka, Judd. "Pair Charged in Death of Wolf." *Arizona Republic,* 10 March 2000, B1.

Steinhart, Peter. *The Company of Wolves.* New York: Alfred A. Knopf, 1995.

Sylvain, Diane. "Coyote Vigil." *High Country News,* 17 April 1997, 14.

Symington, Fife, Governor of Arizona. Letter to Dan Glickman, Secretary of Agriculture. Public Records (March 1997):1–2.

Taugher, Mike. "Wolf was 'Coming Directly' at Clan." *Albuquerque Journal,* 17 June 1998, A1, A6.

——. "Biologists Afraid for Big Bold Wolf." *Albuquerque Journal,* 18 April 1999, A1.

U.S. Congress. *Endangered Species Act of 1973.* 16 U.S.C. 1531–1544, 87 Stat. 884. As amended through 100th Congress. Washington, D.C.: GOP, 1988.

USDA Forest Service. *Wildlife, Fish, and Sensitive Plant Habitat Management.* Title 2600. Washington, D.C.: USDA Forest Service, 1986.

U.S. Department of the Interior, Fish and Wildlife Service. "Endangered and Threatened Wildlife and Plants: Proposed Rule for Proposed Establishment of a Nonessential-Experimental Population of the Mexican Gray Wolf in Arizona and New Mexico." *U.S. Federal Register* 61:85 (May 1, 1996):19237–19248.

——. "Endangered and Threatened Wildlife and Plants: Final Rule for Proposed Establishment of a Nonessential Experimental Population of the Mexican Gray Wolf in Arizona and New Mexico." *U.S. Federal Register* 63:7 (January 12, 1998):1752–1772.

U.S. District Court for the District of New Mexico. *Wolf Action Group et al Plaintiff v The United States, Manuel Lujan et al Defendants.* (Lawsuit) No. CIV 90-0390HB, 1990.

——. *Wolf Action Group et al Plaintiffs v United States, Bruce Babbitt Defendant.* (Stipulated Settlement Agreement) No. CIV 90-0390HB, 1993.

——. *New Mexico Cattle Growers et al Plaintiffs v U.S. Fish and Wildlife Service et al Defendants.* (Complaint) No. CIV-98-275-LH, 1998.

U.S. Fish and Wildlife Service. *Mexican Wolf Recovery Plan.* Albuquerque, N.Mex.: U.S. Fish and Wildlife Service, 1982.

——. *The Mexican Wolf Recovery Program.* Albuquerque, N.Mex.: U.S. Fish and Wildlife Service, 1986.

——. *Reintroduction of the Mexican Wolf within its Historic Range in the Southwestern United States, Draft Environmental Impact Statement.* Albuquerque, N.Mex.: U.S. Fish and Wildlife Service, 1995.

——. *Reintroduction of the Mexican Wolf within its Historic Range in the Southwestern United States, Final Environmental Impact Statement.* Albuquerque, N.Mex.: U.S. Fish and Wildlife Service, 1996.

——. *Notice of Record of Decision and Statement of Findings on the Environmental Impact Statement on Reintroduction of the Mexican Gray Wolf to its Historic Range in the Southwestern United States.* Albuquerque, N.Mex.: U.S. Fish and Wildlife Service, 1997.

——. "Facts about Mexican Wolves Released into Arizona." *Public Affairs* (December 1998):1, 2.

——. *Mexican Wolf Reintroduction Update.* (February 1998–present) (Source for status information on the released Mexican wolves.)

——. Mexican Wolf Reintroduction Press Releases. (February 1998–present) (Source for status information on the released Mexican wolves.)

——. "Killing of a Mexican Wolf by Richard Humphrey." In Report of Investigation. Arlington, Va.: USFWS Division of Law Enforcement, 1998.

Valdez, Linda. "Give That Man a Prize." *The Arizona Republic,* 14 February 1995, B4.

——. "Welcome Back." *The Arizona Republic,* 7 March 1997, B4.

Van Gieson, Judith. *The Wolf Path.* New York: HarperCollins Publishers, 1992.

Williams, Toni. "Rancher Worried About Several Wolf Incidents." *The Copper Era,* 14 April 1999, 1.

Wolf, Tom. "Politics Can't Save Endangered Species." *High Country News,* 26 August 1991, 15.

Wood, Daniel. *Wolves.* Ontario: Whitecap Books, 1994.

Young, Stanley P., and Edward A. Goldman. *The Wolves of North America, Part 1.* Washington, D.C.: American Wildlife Institute, 1944.

Yozwiak, Steve. "Wolves Howl Again in Arizona." *The Arizona Republic,* 27 January 1998, B1–2.

. "2 More Gray Wolves Shot, Killed in Wild." *The Arizona Republic,* 11 November 1998, A1, A20.

——. "Wolf 'Here to Stay,' Babbitt Says." *The Arizona Republic,* 17 November 1998, B1, B6.

——. "5th Wolf Shot to Death." *The Arizona Republic,* 25 November 1998, A1, A20.

Zimen, Eric. *The Wolf: A Species in Danger.* New York: Delacourte, 1984.

Source Credits

Abbey, Edward. From *Beyond the Wall* (pp. 39–40). Copyright © 1971. Holt, Rinehart and Winston. Used by permission.

Boyd-Heger, Diane. From "Living with Wolves," in *Intimate Nature* (p. 92), edited by Linda Hogan, Deena Metzger, and Brenda Peterson. Copyright © 1998. The Ballantine Publishing Group, New York. Used by permission.

Fischer, Hank. From *Wolf Wars: The Remarkable Inside Story of the Restoration of Wolves to Yellowstone* (p. 170). Copyright © 1995. Falcon Press Publishing Co., Inc. Used by permission.

Fox, Michael W. From *The Soul of the Wolf* (p. 106). Copyright © 1980. Little, Brown and Co., Boston/Toronto. Used by permission.

Leopold, Aldo. From *A Sand County Almanac: And Sketches Here and There* (pp. 138, 141). Copyright © 1949, 1977 by Oxford University Press, Inc. Used by permission of Oxford University Press, Inc.

Lopez, Barry. From *Of Wolves and Men* (p. 249). Copyright © 1978. Charles Scribner's Sons, Division of Simon and Schuster, New York. Used by permission.

Mech, L. David. From *The Wolf: The Ecology and Behavior of an Endangered Species* (p. 348). Copyright © 1970. Natural History Press, Doubleday Publishing Company. Used by permission.

Pearce, Joseph Garrison. "Arizona's First Forest Ranger," from *Arizona Memories* (pp. 127, 131–32), edited by Anne Hodges Morgan and Rennard Strickland. Copyright © 1984 by The Arizona Board of Regents. Reprinted by permission of the University of Arizona Press.

Zimen, Eric. From *The Wolf: A Species in Danger* (p. 331). Copyright © 1981. Dell Publishing, a division of Random House, Inc., New York. Used by permission.

Index

About the Author

Bobbie Holaday has been credited with spearheading the citizen effort behind the U.S. Fish and Wildlife Service and the Arizona Game and Fish Department program to reintroduce the endangered Mexican wolf to the Blue Range Area of Arizona and New Mexico. In 1987, she founded Preserve Arizona's Wolves (P.A.WS.).

Long a wilderness advocate, Holaday was responsible for two major wilderness designations in Arizona: the Hells Gate Wilderness and the Eagletail Mountains Wilderness.

Holaday, now in her eighties, received her bachelor's degree in English from Denison University, Granville, Ohio, in 1944, and later took graduate courses at Arizona State University. During World War II, she joined the U.S. Navy WAVEs and served as a pharmacist mate in a Naval Hospital. Following the birth of two daughters, she found employment with several large corporations, including twenty-eight years with the computer department of General Electric Company, which later merged with Honeywell. Holaday wrote countless technical manuals and user guides before working as a systems analyst.

She wrote and edited *PAW PRINTS*, P.A.WS.'s quarterly newsletter, and has had wolf articles published in *WOLF! Magazine*; *The Howler*, magazine of the Wolf Society of Great Britain; and the Arizona Sierra Club's *Canyon Echo*. She has written for the *Arizona Republic, Tribune Newspapers* and the *Sierra Vista Herald*. In 1983, she self-published a small volume of poetry titled *Wild Places*.

The author's awards include the 1994 Volunteer Service Award from the Arizona Heritage Alliance, the Arizona Game and Fish Commission's 1995 Environmentalist of the Year, and the Defenders of Wildlife's Conservation Award for Excellence in 1998.